Secular
Humanism:
Threat and Challenge

Secular Humanism:
Threat and Challenge

Robert E. Webber

ZONDERVAN
PUBLISHING HOUSE OF THE ZONDERVAN CORPORATION
GRAND RAPIDS, MICHIGAN 49506

Secular Humanism: Threat and Challenge
Copyright © 1982 by The Zondervan Corporation

Library of Congress Cataloging in Publication Data

Webber, Robert.
    Secular humanism, threat and challenge.

    Bibliography: p.
    1. Secularism—United States. 2. Humanism. 3. United States—Moral
conditions. 4. Church and the world. I. Title.

BL2747.8.W42 1982   211'.6'0973   82-8320
ISBN 0-310-36670-4   AACR2

Edited by James E. Ruark
Designed by Louise Bauer

Printed in the United States of America

To my brother
Ken
for faithful service
at Christ's Home
since 1960

Contents

Acknowledgments

It is always impossible to acknowledge all the people who play an important part in producing a book. However; I owe a special debt of gratitude to people who were supportive, encouraging, and helpful. Thanks goes to Dr. Ward Kriegbaum, academic vice-president of Wheaton College, for financial help to cover the costs of research and typing. A special debt of gratitude is owed to students Wendy Georges and Ellen Davis for tracking down the articles and books that I needed. And the manuscript could not have been completed without the important help of typists Mary Lou McCurdy, Jane Marston, and Karen Mason.

I especially want to acknowledge the editorial and organizational skills of Nance Wabshaw. Her insights and suggestions have helped make the book readable to the layperson.

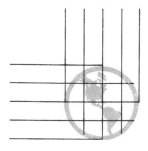

1
Introduction

THE PROBLEM

Something has happened to America in the last two decades. No matter whom you talk to—ministers, teachers, doctors, lawyers, housewives, blue-collar or white-collar workers—most seem to agree a change has taken place, and it's not a welcomed change.

"It's a permissive society," a mother of three children said pensively. "I don't like the temptations my children have to face—it's a tough world in which to grow up." "Yes," a young couple echo the thought. "We're not sure we want to bring children into this society."

What is it that has made our society change in the last two decades? Why do many people feel uneasy about the future? What is the cause of the upsurge in free sex, abortion, incest, pornography, the threat of nuclear war, government control, invasion of privacy, distortion of the news, inflation, and unemployment?

SECULAR HUMANISM

Secular humanism is to blame, say the religious leaders of the new right! It is leading us right down the primrose path of destruction. And unless we do something to stop it, things will get worse! "Secular humanism has become the religion of America." It has "taken the place of the Bible," says Jerry Falwell, founder and president of the Moral Majority.

There are "275,000 humanists" who control every-

thing in the United States including the Supreme
Court, the federal government, public education, labor
unions, and the media, says Tim LaHaye, the author of
the book *The Battle for the Mind.* We must, he insists,
remove these people from their positions of power and
influence and replace them with moral people, preferably born-again Christians.[1]

REACTION TO SECULAR HUMANISM

The religious nature of secular humanism has led
a number of writers to take up the pen against it, including fundamentalists, evangelicals, Roman Catholics, and Orthodox Christians.

"It's the most dangerous religion in America," fundamentalist Homer Duncan writes in his book *Secular
Humanism.*[2] Evangelical philosopher Francis A.
Schaeffer writes in his latest book, *A Christian Manifesto,* that secular humanism has caused "a fundamental change in the overall way people think and view
the world and life as a whole."[3] A Catholic theologian
and writer, Thomas Molnar, regards secular humanism as "an alternative to monotheistic religion, the expression of a man-centered worldview."[4] The Russian
writer Aleksandr Solzhenitsyn declared in his famous
address at Harvard in 1978, that humanism has sent
"modern western civilization on the dangerous trend to
worship man and his material need."[5]

What is the meaning of all these statements? Is
secular humanism nothing more than "sound and fury
signifying nothing," to use Shakespeare's phrase, that
some claim it is? Or ought we to share the concern
voiced by C. S. Lewis? He suggested that at one time
history was divided into two periods, the pre-Christian
and the Christian. But he said that more recently "it
falls into three—the pre-Christian, the Christian and
the post-Christian."[6] Could all the current noise be a
reaction to a decline in Christian influence, a sense

that Christian memory is lost in the West, that a process has occurred by which the Western world has indeed become "post-Christian"?

THE SECULARIZATION OF THE WEST

Many scholars argue that the West has undergone a process of secularization which has brought us into the post-Christian era dominated by secular humanism.

Bernard E. Meland, professor emeritus in theology from the University of Chicago Divinity School, defines secularization in this way: It is a movement *away from* "an historical order of life that presupposes religious sanctions"; it is a movement *toward* something—"a new community of mind emerging, centering around new disciplines and forms of inquiry that were to challenge and eventually to supersede this prevailing Christian consensus"; and finally it is "a *condition of life* that steadily invades the processes of society and family life, feeding upon the apathy and indifference of people to historic sensibilities and religious principles."[7]

All three of these stages are painfully evident in Western history. Many Christians and non-Christians alike agree with C. S. Lewis that we are living in a post-Christian era.

In America, the social order has been breaking away from its Christian roots (i.e., the impact Christianity has had on social institutions in the West since Constantine). Consequently Christianity has gradually retreated from the political, economic, legal, and scientific realms of life. At the same time, a less significant role has emerged for religion. It has become privatized, retreating into the inner person or finding definition in personal religious acts. As a result, Christianity has become increasingly divorced from the social order. (Figure 1 illustrates this process.)

There are some who welcome this change in soci-

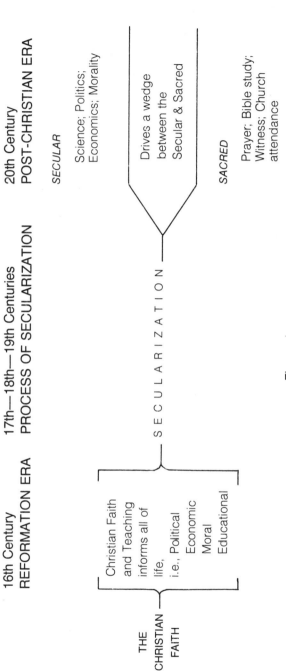

16th Century
REFORMATION ERA

17th—18th—19th Centuries
PROCESS OF SECULARIZATION

20th Century
POST-CHRISTIAN ERA

SECULAR

Science; Politics;
Economics; Morality

Drives a wedge
between the
Secular & Sacred

SACRED

Prayer; Bible study;
Witness; Church
attendance

S E C U L A R I Z A T I O N

Christian Faith
and Teaching
informs all of
life,
i.e., Political
Economic
Moral
Educational

THE
CHRISTIAN
FAITH

Figure 1

ety. For them religion, which they view as false, is gradually being replaced by science, which they regard as true. To them, science now offers the answers to the origin of man and his meaning; religion is relegated to myth and fantasy. The Christian religion *once was* the force that gave shape to our societal values, but it is no longer. A new mind-set has emerged that now gives a different shape to our values.

If this process of secularization is true, then all the alarms sounded by people like Jerry Falwell, Tim LaHaye, Francis Schaeffer, Thomas Molnar, and Aleksandr Solzhenitsyn are grounded in a basic truth: *Our society has undergone a drastic change. Even Christians have been affected by the change—making a separation between the secular and the sacred in their own lives.*

The most obvious evidence of this separation between the secular and the sacred among Christians is found in our elevation of things spiritual and our subsequent indifference toward the "nonspiritual" or neutral areas of life. For example, some act as though the spiritual life consists of prayer, Bible reading, and church attendance while vocation and matters of public policy are nonspiritual concerns. For this reason many Christians have abdicated their responsibility as citizens to exercise a spiritual influence over all of life. Relegating spirituality to the "inner life," or to the "secret chambers of life," or to vocations of ministry (in the sense of church-related work) we have failed to fulfill our calling before God in other aspects of public life such as politics, social welfare, business, the humanities, and the like.

Christians have to face the fact that a great majority of people (including our fellow Christians) no longer live by an overall Christian structure of thought and values. Gone are the days when Christianity was the major influence providing stability to the social order and producing thinkers like Augustine, Aquinas, or Calvin; or art like the Eastern icons or the Sistine Chapel paintings of Michelangelo; or music like the Gregorian Chant or that of Bach or Handel's *Messiah;* or literature like that of Milton or Dante. The new forces unleashed by the Renaissance, the Enlightenment, the Industrial Revolution, the evolutionary hypothesis, and technological advances have changed the shape of society. The influence of Christianity has dissipated considerably, and secularism is now a major competitor of it.

It is no longer possible for a particular consensus to claim a monopoly on society. The Christian church and its point of view is only *one among many* making our present situation a veritable marketplace of worldviews which are simultaneously in competition. Atheists, Christians, Satanists, mystics, socialists, capitalists, skeptics, and members of various cults work side by side. This is a relatively new phenomenon in American society. In the midst of all this confusion some new leaders have emerged to suggest ways to deal with the problem of secularization.

CAN SECULARIZATION BE REVERSED?

The emergence of leaders like Jerry Falwell and Tim LaHaye is probably no surprise to sociologist Peter Berger, who predicted it as early as 1977.

"Intellectuals like to anticipate historic moments," he wrote in *Facing Up to Modernity,* "and some of my observations suggest that the Christian community in America might be on the eve of such a 'historic moment.'" What Berger predicted was a "powerful reversal of the secularization process." Almost like a prophet of old, he looked into the future and foresaw a regeneration of the fundamental values of society and argued that the only force in American society capable of accomplishing such a reversal is Christianity.[8]

But what kind of Christianity will introduce this reversal? Berger claims change will come from *the authority of those who have come to terms with their own experience and who are convinced that, in however imperfect a measure, they have grasped some important truths about the human condition* (emphasis added). These leaders will come from neither the extreme right nor the extreme left, Berger says. The new religious right seems bent on "cleaning up America" through moral legislation and power politics, while the extreme left seems to fall all over itself at tempting to be "relevant" to modern man. The left offers a watered-down Christianity that has lost its supernatural roots, reducing Christianity to little more than a moral do-goodism or your friendly institution prepared to support the latest liberation fad whether it is the sexual revolution or ordination of homosexuals.

Peter Berger has spoken eloquently into our situation in America. Amid the voices from the right and the voices from the left, we need to rediscover an authentic Christian humanism that can influence the social order without recourse to power politics on the one hand, or an accommodation to fadism on the other.

AUTHENTIC CHRISTIAN HUMANISM

This is a book about the recovery of an authentic Christian humanism and its confrontation with secular humanism. In the forthcoming chapters a number of complex issues will be addressed for the purpose of informing Christians of the struggle that lies ahead. To remain clear about the issues, let us keep the following points in mind:

Secularization has driven a wedge between religious faith and our life in the world.

The unfortunate result of secularization is that it has put the church in a position of retreat and forced Christians to privatize their faith. Consequently Christianity has become what Abraham Kuyper, the former prime minister of Holland, once called "a religion of the closet."

Secular humanism is a potent force in the United States of America.

Secular humanism is a viewpoint that competes against Christianity. It is the view of life or frame of reference that now informs what we Christians incorrectly call the "secular" part of life. It rejects the existence of a personal God who created the world, revealed Himself in history, and came in the person of Jesus Christ to save the world. Therefore it offers a different answer to the Big Questions of life such as "Where did I come from?" and "What is the meaning of life?" and "How should I live?"

The extreme of the religious right does not have the answer.

The religious right tends to lump all humanists together, failing to make distinctions between various kinds of humanists and their potential effect on society. Furthermore, they call for the Christianizing of America through legislation and political clout. Although this approach may have an immediate effect, it will not stand up over the long term.

The extreme of the religious left does not have the answer.

In the last decade or two, the religious left has practically abandoned support of Christian morality. In their concern to fight for the oppressed and those on the underside of society—a proper concern—they appear to support not only the sinner, but the sin. In their desire to be compassionate, they offer little help to a society whose overpermissiveness may lead it into self-destruction.

The alternative to the religious right and religious left is the recovery of an authentic Christian humanism.

I
The
Humanist
Debate

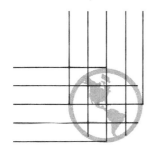

2
What Is Humanism?

"Humanism challenges every principle on which America was founded. It advocates abortion on demand, recognition of homosexuals, free use of pornography, legalizing of prostitution and gambling, and free use of drugs, among other things," says Jerry Falwell.[1]

Not so, say other Christians: These charges are being erroneously laid at the feet of humanism. "They've taken another perfectly good word, narrowed its range of meaning, and are swinging it like a club in all directions," says Richard McCartney, editor of the Southern Baptist newspaper in Oklahoma.[2]

One who is swinging hard is Leo Wine of Ashland, Oregon. In a series of radio programs he told his hearers exactly what humanism is doing and where it is taking us.

Humanists, Wine said, are "promoting sexual perversion." They are doing so "because they want to create such an obsession with sex among our young people that they will have no time or interest for spiritual pursuits." Humanists are "leading us toward the chaos of the French Revolution." "They will," Wine categorically states, "name their own dictator who will create out of the ashes of our pro-moral republic a humanist utopia, an atheistic, socialistic, amoral humanist society for America and the rest of the world. In fact, their goal is to accomplish that takeover by or before the year 2000."[3]

Unfortunately, the characterization of humanism by spokespersons like Jerry Falwell and Leo Wine is all too common today. Is that really what humanism is about? Or, are these speakers giving us a caricature of humanism that is only half right?

HUMANISM DEFINED

The term *humanism* refers to man and expresses his importance. All humanists, whether religious or nonreligious, agree that man and his welfare on earth is a matter of central interest. More than two thousand years ago the Roman playwright Terence captured the spirit of humanism in his saying, "I am a man, and nothing human is foreign to me."[4]

Humanism also has to do with the arts. It has a sharp and robust interest in what man is able to create, especially as a result of his mind. Humanist literature focuses in particular on such things as the astuteness of man's mind and the mystery of his psyche. For example, Geoffrey Chaucer of England tells humorous stories in his *Canterbury Tales* that demonstrate his keen insight into the complexities of human nature. Thomas More, the devout churchman and Christian humanist, holds forth high moral and social ideals for humanity in his work *Utopia*. Humanist artists developed special techniques to emphasize the beauty and symmetry of the body and to capture the details of nature and life. Michelangelo created realistic, detailed, and highly individualized statues like *David* and realistic human personalities like those depicted in the Sistine Chapel.

Education is another focus of humanism. Humanists have great ideals for the educated man, what we call today the "Renaissance man." Such a person is to learn, as Matthew Arnold said in the nineteenth century, "the best that has been thought and said in the world." He is to be the "ideal gentleman," skilled in art, music, literature, and athletics and able to be an engaging conversationalist in economic and political matters as well as issues of worldly interest. Indeed, this has been the goal of an education centering in the humanities. Colleges and universities train students in religion, philosophy, language, literature, art, music, and history as a means to make them well-rounded and intelligent human beings. Certainly the leaders of today's religious right should have no quarrel with this kind of humanism.

THE ORIGIN OF HUMANISM

The roots of humanism are found in the Greco-Roman world and in the Judaic Christian heritage (see figure 2).

In the Greco-Roman world, humanism was first articulated by Protagoras, a Greek philosopher of the fifth century B.C., when he proclaimed that "man is the measure of all things." But even in the ancient world there were fundamental differences of opinion between thinkers on what is good for men and what isn't good for man and how one can know these truths.

Plato, for example, maintained that the good life was discoverable and the same for everyone. Put another way, Plato argued that goodness which exists independently of men can be discovered and taught. Plato believed in moral absolutism. For him, morality was not a "matter of opinion" or "personal preference." There are, he insisted, moral absolutes that exist independently of man or even of a superior being. Man can discover these "rights" and "wrongs" through the power of his intellect. Then he must discipline and train himself to live by these precepts. This, for Plato, is the good life.

On the other hand, Aristotle believed the good life could be discovered through observation. He noticed, for example, that all the people of his day who led a good life had one common characteristic: happiness. Happiness, Aristotle concluded, is not a static state of being, but a dynamic quality of life that accompanies

THE ORIGIN AND DEVELOPMENT OF HUMANISM

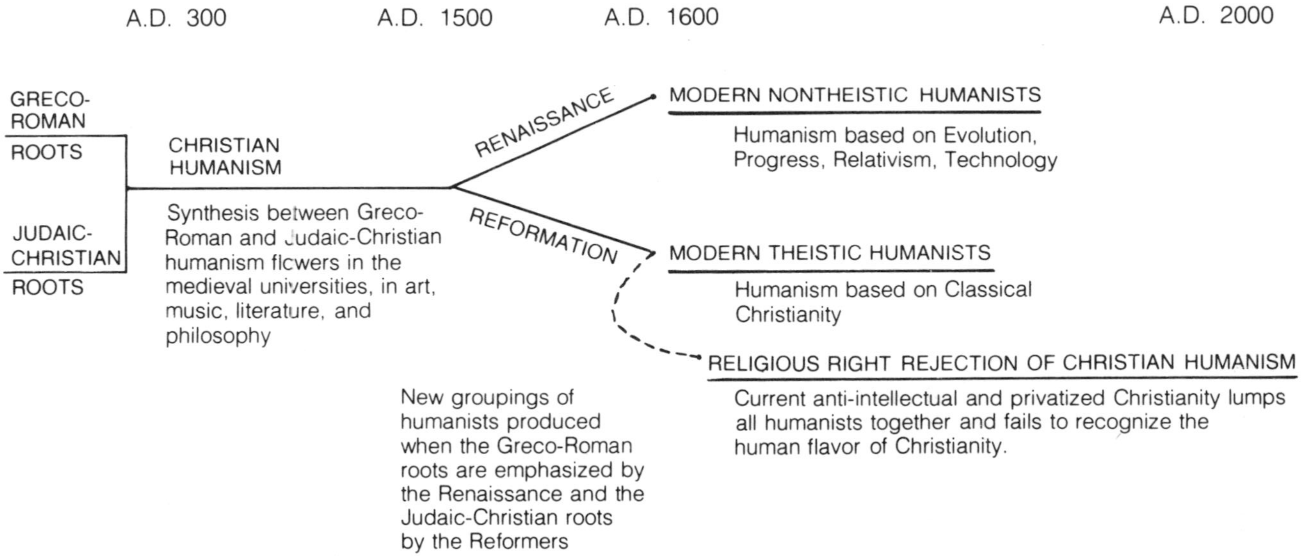

A.D. 300   A.D. 1500   A.D. 1600   A.D. 2000

GRECO-
ROMAN
ROOTS

JUDAIC-
CHRISTIAN
ROOTS

CHRISTIAN
HUMANISM

Synthesis between Greco-
Roman and Judaic-Christian
humanism flowers in the
medieval universities, in art,
music, literature, and
philosophy

RENAISSANCE

REFORMATION

New groupings of
humanists produced
when the Greco-Roman
roots are emphasized by
the Renaissance and the
Judaic-Christian roots
by the Reformers

MODERN NONTHEISTIC HUMANISTS

Humanism based on Evolution,
Progress, Relativism, Technology

MODERN THEISTIC HUMANISTS

Humanism based on Classical
Christianity

RELIGIOUS RIGHT REJECTION OF CHRISTIAN HUMANISM

Current anti-intellectual and privatized Christianity lumps
all humanists together and fails to recognize the
human flavor of Christianity.

Figure 2

man's life. So if a man enjoys eating or intellectual pursuits or friendships, happiness is the quality of life that accompanies these activities. But how should man behave to achieve this happiness? Aristotle's answer lay in his famous formula "the doctrine of the golden mean": the correct amount always lies between too much and too little. For Aristotle, then, the good life was found by each person as he found his own "mean." Thus Aristotle is a relativist. The "mean" is not the same for everyone; the good life is different from person to person.

In spite of the differences between Plato and Aristotle, it is fair to say that both advocated principles of discipline, virtue, wisdom, loyalty, and justice.

The second source of humanism is found in the Judaic-Christian heritage. "Biblical Humanism," writes C. Hassell Bullock, professor of Old Testament at Wheaton College, "is identifiable in Proverbs, Ecclesiastes, and the Song of Songs. Man probes his world, searches his own mind, rationalizes about the meaning of human existence and the absurdity of death. No relationship however obscure, no phenomenon however small and insignificant is unworthy of examination."[5]

The New Testament's emphasis on man is equally strong. Mark Noll, professor of history at Wheaton College, has written, "At the heart [of the Christian faith] stands the confession that God—the originator of everything right and good—himself became man."[6] The extreme fundamentalists who castigate humanism so easily need this gentle reminder that God himself lived in his world as a human being. Because of this fact, being human and being concerned about human things are basic to Christian humanism.

But there is a difference between Greco-Roman humanism and Judeo-Christian humanism. One is naturalistic and the other is supernatural. This is the central dividing line. On this point the clash of systems is bound to occur.

THE DEVELOPMENT OF CHRISTIAN HUMANISM

The development of Christian humanism is a long and complex story. For that reason it can be told here only in broad strokes, enabling the reader to see the shifts that have occurred through the centuries.

It must be kept in mind that the Incarnation and its radical implications for humans and humanitarian principles come to fruition in a society that was decidedly secular. Thomas Molnar says of the origins of Christian humanism, "Born in the pagan civilization of the Hellenistic-Roman world, Christianity reacted to the prevailing views, systems, and assumptions, in other words to the intellectual environment."[7]

Christianity was faced with a challenge that was every bit as difficult as the one we face today. The surrounding culture promoted belief in many gods, and these gods were all distant and incapable of relating to man. A cardinal doctrine of paganism was its insistence that the immaterial could not participate in the material. Therefore God—or gods—could not experience human existence and could not relate to the pain and suffering of humanity.

The Christian proclamation that it was *God who became man* in Jesus Christ broke through the pagan indifference of the gods and established the notion of a god who became human, a god who experienced humanity and cared about the human situation. This notion held radical implications for pagan culture.

For example, the doctrine of the Incarnation asserts that God is knowable. Paganism has no adequate concept of a God who revealed himself or even cared enough to reveal himself. But Christianity made the revolutionary claim that God Almighty, the Creator of heaven and earth, is actually knowable.

God, the Christians claimed, had made himself known in history through the people of Israel, in the law (which set forth the boundaries of a good existence), and finally in Jesus Christ, in whom God modeled true humanity.

Furthermore, the doctrine of the Incarnation affirmed the dignity of man through its teaching that the man Jesus Christ is the express image of God (see Colossians 1:15; Hebrews 1:3). This doctrine of the Incarnation connected with the Old Testament teaching that human beings are made in the image of God, led the early Christians into an affirmation that all human life is sacred. A case in point is found in the Roman world, where abortion was freely accepted as a means of population control or a convenience for those who did not want a child. Children who were born with deficiencies were subject to infanticide. These children were simply taken to the woods or a desert place and left there to die.

But the Christians were characterized by a radically different lifestyle. In the *Didache* ("Teaching"), a document that some scholars date as early as A.D. 50, Christians were told not to "murder a child by abortion."[8] Aristides described Christians in his *Apology* by saying, "They love one another and from widows they do not turn away their esteem; and they deliver the orphan from him who treats him harshly."[9] The dignity in which Christians held human life stood in sharp contrast to the average pagan indifference to human life.

The doctrine of the Incarnation also made an impact on human behavior because it affirmed that moral absolutes were revealed. Such an idea was unpopular in pagan culture. Although Plato and Aristotle taught virtue and discipline and called on people to live a good life, the concept of revealed morals were foreign to Hellenistic thought.

Consequently Christianity gave birth to a more clear-cut notion of right and wrong and had a *basis* from which people could arrive at their conclusions. The Gentiles who came into the church had to be taught these morals because they did not have the advantage of the Jewish background and its training in values. But the revolution of morals introduced by the Christian, based on the law and the model of Christ who fulfilled the law in every way, made an impact on the society through Christians who adopted this new radical lifestyle. A typical example may be cited from the second-century *Epistle to Diognetus*, in which the anonymous author said of Christians, "They share their bread with each other, but not their marriage bed."[10]

Finally, the church acting as the extension of Christ in the world made a significant impact on the social and political order of the ancient and medieval world. The notion that there is a transcendent God who created the world, made man in his image, entered into history to destroy the powers of evil, established the church as an expression of his presence in the world, and guides history to its consummation proved to be a group of radical ideas with significant political, economic, and moral consequences.

The consequences of these ideas brought the great Roman Empire to its knees. This empire under Nero, Domitian, and Decius had attempted to destroy the Christian church; but then, during the time of Constantine, in the early fourth century A.D., it became captive to Christian teaching and influence. Paganism was gradually replaced by Christianity as emperors and citizens alike acknowledged the claim of a sovereign Lord over their personal and public lives. Christian leaders like Ambrose, the Bishop of Milan; John Chrysostom, the Bishop of Constantinople; and Augustine, the Bishop of Hippo, exercised a powerful influence in both the church and public policy. Christians permeated every vocational aspect of life— business, politics, education, and the arts. An authentic Christian humanism had been born—a Christianity which sought to apply its teaching in every sphere of living.

Unfortunately Christian humanism can also go astray. A hint of the future problem is already seen by A.D. 380 in a decree issued by Emperor Theodosius that made Christianity the only legal religion in the Roman Empire and placed dissidents under the condemnation of the state. The problem became more acute in the high medieval period when the church promoted Holy Crusades and inquisitions as means of maintaining an external Christendom.

It is highly doubtful that Constantine or the bishops of Rome in the early fourth century could have anticipated such a perversion of Christian humanism. Nevertheless, it occurred—and its existence prompts us to ask some serious questions about the relationship of an authentic Christian humanism to a fallen society.

THE SPLIT BETWEEN RENAISSANCE AND REFORMATION HUMANISM

The corruption of the late medieval church nearly extinguished the light of Christian humanism. At the same time the rise of the Renaissance and Reformation coincided with the decline of the Roman church as a moral force and political power in the fifteenth and sixteenth centuries. The sources for this radical change in history were the European rediscovery of the Greco-Roman world and the world of early Christianity, which came about when Greek and early church manuscripts were retrieved from Constantinople after its fall to the Turks in A.D. 1453.

For our study, the most important contribution of

these manuscripts is the rediscovery of the Greco-Roman humanism. Subsequently Greek humanism was reasserted through the Renaissance humanists, who became imitators of the humanism of Greece and Rome. These humanists were breaking away from the medieval habit of mind and the medieval ideal of a corporate society and were moving toward individualism and the assertion of self.

"Exuberant humanists" is the term given to them by Harvard historian Crane Brinton. "They were humanists in the sense that they believed that man is the measure of all things, and that each man is a measure of himself," Brinton writes. "They were men who dared to be themselves, because they trusted in their own natural powers, in something inside themselves. They were the kind of men we Americans like, men with no stuffiness, men who might almost have come from Texas."[11]

MODERN NONTHEISTIC HUMANISTS

These Renaissance thinkers were forerunners of the modern nontheistic humanists of today. Their spirit of exuberance and the conviction that man is the center of all things gradually became hardened into dogma as it was filtered through the doctrine of the essential goodness of man, the convictions of a nontheistic evolution, and the utopian hope of a doctrine of progress which promises humankind that things after all are really getting better and better all the time.

Contemporary nontheistic humanism is distinguished by four characteristics, according to Paul Kurtz, the editor of *The Humanist* and professor of philosophy at the state university of New York at Buffalo. These are confidence in man; opposition to supernaturalism; faith in science, reason, and experience; and humanitarianism.[12]

Confidence in Man

Humanists believe in the dogma of development which teaches that mankind continually grows out of a need to depend on the past. This means that our current view of life must break away from all religious dogma, and our ideals must be under constant scrutiny in the light of present needs and social demands.

At the heart of this assertion lies the conviction expressed by the humanist J. H. Randall that "the faith that alone promises salvation is the faith in intelligence."[10] This does not mean, however, that humanists do not frequently come to values similar to Christian values through the intellect.

Fundamentalists who read a statement like Randall's immediately see an *active* humanist movement intentionally determined to destroy all Christian values. For this reason they agree with LaHaye that humanists have "brainwashed millions of Christians."[14] LaHaye is correct that this view poses a threat, but fortunately there are many humanists like Khoren Arisian, a leader of the New York Society for Ethical Culture, who will not allow humanist assumptions to be carried to their logical conclusions, but rather insist that "life is always larger than logic."[15] Many humanists live, like Socrates, by traditional values despite the contradiction their own system implies.

Opposition to Supernaturalism

It comes as no surprise that nontheistic humanists categorically reject all Christian creeds and dogmas and regard them as impediments to human growth. Humanists argue that religious views lock people into an inferior stage of development. Religious people, they claim, allow themselves to live by principles from the outside which are *imposed* upon them rather than living by rules that come from personal conviction. Fortunately, humanists in general do not advocate the tearing down of our moral structure and the introduction of a complete freedom for man "to do whatever he wants to do whenever he wants to do it." Unfortunately, when and if a totalitarianism from the right or the left arises to destroy man's freedom, the humanists' rejection of a supernatural God and the authority of revealed principles for living leaves them without any basis to call evil, evil other than an ineffective appeal to "human experience."

Faith in Science, Reason, and Experience

The humanists reject revelational values and search for values *within the created order,* preferably from human experience. According to the humanist philosopher Antony Flew, "To adopt such a scientific approach unreservedly is to accept as ultimate in all matters of fact and real existence the appeal to the evidence of experience alone."[16]

Another humanist, Roywood Sellars, suggests that "there is a new orientation in our culture under way" and reminds us "there is much to be done in the domain of human values, personal and social. The human spirit must concentrate on its table of values and define the spiritual in this context. It is a demanding and worthy task."[17] In other words, because the humanist has confidence in man and his ability to solve problems through science, reason, and experience, we can live with a positive and optimistic hope in the future.

Humanitarianism

Humanism supports the development of a society that contains as much diversity in values as is reasonable. It wants to avoid imposing a single, narrow point of view upon all people. It espouses a freedom for each person to fulfill his or her destiny with as little resistance as possible. For that reason humanism is for man—it has the best interests of the human race in mind and wants to support those attitudes and programs that will alleviate suffering and help people achieve their full potential.

CHRISTIAN HUMANISM

Although Christian humanism has suffered a significant loss of influence over the past four centuries, the viewpoint is still held by many Christians around the world. Christian humanism may be contrasted to humanism in the following four convictions: confidence in God in Christ; a supernatural world-view; the power of Christ acting through the church; and incarnational humanitarianism.

Confidence in God in Christ

"It is my own conviction that the incarnation of Christ sanctifies life and gives the ground for an understanding of human values," writes Wayne K. Clymer, a bishop in the United Methodist Church.[18]

This same theme was expressed in "A Christian Humanist Manifesto" recently published in *Eternity* magazine, a well-known voice within evangelical circles. The authors protested in the preamble that "in our time the word 'humanism' has been claimed by those who explain human existence without any reference to God." They added that "the proper study of mankind is not man alone, but God and man together." It is, of course, in Jesus Christ where God and man come together so that Jesus is, as the manifesto declares, "the model of true humanness for all generations."[19]

A significant implication of the Incarnation is that God came to this world because of a dehumanizing element at work in the created order. The origin of this element is already depicted in the account of the Fall. Man has made a choice to make something other than

God his god. So Paul states in Romans 1:25 that God's creatures "exchanged the truth of God for a lie, and worshiped and served created things rather than the creator." In that same passage Paul gives a description of a culture that has forsaken God. He says that they have turned toward "shameful lusts," they "abandoned natural relations," and they have "a depraved mind" becoming filled "with every kind of wickedness, evil, greed and depravity. They are full of envy, murder, strife, deceit and malice. They are gossips, slanderers, God-haters, insolent, arrogant and boastful; they invent ways of doing evil; they disobey their parents; they are senseless, faithless, heartless, ruthless" (Rom. 1:26-31).

Here Paul clearly describes the Greco-Roman culture into which God became incarnate. It is also a description that fits Western culture today. Yet God was *for* the culture. He came not to condemn it, but to save it. Christian humanism, taking its cue from the Incarnation, is concerned to infuse new life into the culture. It is not satisfied to condemn alone; rather, it seeks to regenerate the culture by humanizing it.

A Supernatural World-View

The purpose of God's incarnation in Jesus Christ was to die for the sins of the world and through that death destroy death, sin, and the dominion of the devil. In Ephesians, Paul summarizes the source from which all the evils of the world derive. "Our struggle," he writes, "is not against flesh and blood, but against the rulers, against the authorities, against the powers of this dark world and against the spiritual forces of evil in the heavenly realms" (6:12).

Christian humanism acknowledges a real cosmic battle between light and darkness, good and evil, God and Satan. It claims that God has come in Jesus Christ to destroy the "powers" of evil which dehumanize God's creatures and seek to destroy God's good creation. For this reason, the Incarnation must always be understood in relation to the death, resurrection, and the second coming of Christ.

In death, Christ destroyed the "powers" of evil that brought his creation under the power of death and the dominion of Satan. So Paul wrote to the Christians at Colossae that Christ "disarmed the powers and authorities" and "made a public spectacle of them, triumphing over them by the cross" (Col. 2:15).

In the resurrection, Christ demonstrated his power to recreate in his new body, which was seen by his disciples and many others as a living declaration of his power over death and the grave. In Christ the old creation has gone and a new one has come (2 Cor. 5:17). In Christ we are able to die to "the basic principles of this world" (Col. 2:20); to put to death "whatever belongs to your earthly nature: sexual immorality, impurity, lust, evil desires and greed" (Col. 3:5). We have "put on the new self, which is being renewed in knowledge in the image of its Creator" (Col. 3:10). These admonitions point to the new set of values and principles that belong to the Christian. These are the values of peace, love, compassion, kindness, humility, gentleness, patience, and a host of other qualities that define the humanness of the believer in Jesus Christ. In this sense, *a Christian is a radical humanist, because his life represents a drastic change from those who "walk after the flesh."*

In spite of the death and resurrection of Christ in which sin was defeated, evil still seems to be the rule of the world. Our world is still filled with war, violence, hate, greed, lust, and the like. What of that? Is the Christian vision false? Has there been no effect on the world as a result of the death and resurrection of its Creator and Redeemer? To these questions, the Christian humanist has two answers. The first is that the work of Christ over evil will not be complete until his second coming and judgment, when all evil will be put away forever (see Rev. 22). The second is that the church is the presence of the future in the world now and has the responsibility to function as "salt" and "light" in the world, alleviating it of its pain and acting on its behalf.

The Power of Christ Acting Through the Church

I often ask my students, "Where is Christ?" and they invariably answer, "Sitting on the right hand of the Father."

"Right," I say, "but where is Christ in the world? Where can you see, feel, touch, and relate to him now, today?"

I'm amazed at how few, if any, of these students are able to say, "In the church." Somehow the ancient and Reformational notion that Christ is present to the world in and through the church has been lost to this generation of evangelical Christians. Yet this truth is gradually being recovered by those who are seeking to regain the meaning and practice of what it means to be the "body of Christ" or the "household of faith."

This view of the church is an indispensable part of an authentic Christian humanism. It insists that Christ continues to be present in and to the world through the church, which is an extension of his humanizing presence in the world. So the church, like Jesus, is called to love the world, to serve the world, and to care for the needs of those who are broken and needy.

Incarnational Humanitarianism

The clear teaching of the practical portions of the New Testament epistles and the conviction of the early church fathers is incarnational humanitarianism. Ignatius, the second-century bishop of Antioch who was martyred for his faith, wrote to the church at Smyrna and told them to be wary of those who had wrong notions about the grace of Jesus Christ: "They care nothing about love; they have no concern for widows or orphans, for the oppressed, for those in prison or released, for the hungry or the thirsty."[20]

Incarnational humanitarianism begins with the church. Bishop Clymer expressed it this way: "Beware of those who disparage human life and human values. It is said that Jesus 'became one of us.' This human life is precious. It has the capacity to be incarnated by God. Beware of those who speak much of God, but dismiss concern for the poor of the earth, the reduction of armaments, the conservation of the good earth, God's earth, as humanism. We do not exalt God by denigrating human beings."[21]

A Christian humanist cannot be indifferent to the problems of environment, to the possibilities of nuclear war, or to the cries of the hungry. This pain belongs to the world that the Father has created and cared enough to become part of in Jesus Christ.

In summary, authentic Christian humanism is deeply rooted in the Incarnation, which affirms the love the Father has for being human and for human needs. It acknowledges the sinful condition of humanity and the culture that people unfold. It affirms that sin and its effects have been overcome by the death and resurrection of Christ. It assures us that Christ continues to be present to the world in and through the church, which carries on the ministry of humanizing man and his culture until the Second Coming, when the creation will be brought to its perfection.

The fact that many Christian opponents of humanism seem to be unaware of Christian humanism is a tragic commentary on the anti-intellectual nature of those who have reduced the Christian faith to slogans and a handy list of do's and don'ts. Charles Krauthammer tells the story of a group of Alabama parents complaining to the school board about a history text referring to Erasmus as a "Christian humanist." One critic asked, "How can a Christian be a humanist? . . . If you embrace the humanist manifesto, you embrace that there is no God."[22] The critic was marked more by zeal than by knowledge.

Unfortunately, these kinds of statements are heralded in the media as examples of evangelical stupidity. We must go beyond such an uninformed view of things if we wish to make a positive contribution to our society. Conversely, nontheistic humanism is no friend of Christianity, and to assume that it is, is equally naïve.

SUMMARY

These are the basic ideas to remember from this chapter:

- The central concern of humanism is man and his welfare.

- The roots of humanism lie in the Greco-Roman world and in the Judaic-Christian emphasis on mankind and human values.

- By the fifth century, Christianity had converted the Roman Empire and established a Christian humanism, making a powerful impact on the moral, political, social, educational, and artistic spheres of society.

- The divergent roots of humanism flowered once again as a result of the sixteenth-century Renaissance and Reformation. These two movements were the forerunners of the nontheistic and theistic forms of humanism of the twentieth century.

- Christians are waking up to the threat of a society based on a nontheistic humanism. The alternative is not a deprecation of humanism, but a rediscovery of an authentic Christian humanism.

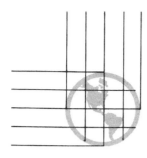

3

What Is Secular Humanism?

We have observed that there are two distinct lines of humanism: the nontheistic and the theistic. Secular humanism, the subject of this chapter, belongs to the nontheistic family of humanism.

It should not come as a surprise to discover there are many different kinds of humanism in the nontheistic family. Among them are ethical humanism, existen tial humanism, scientific humanism, utilitarian humanism, and others.[1] Although all these forms of humanism have certain elements in common, each one is distinguished by a special emphasis. One of the special features of secular humanism is its evangelistic fervor for atheism. For this reason it is not uncommon for opponents of secular humanism to refer to it as *atheistic* humanism.

A SECULAR HUMANIST DECLARATION

In October 1980, sixty-one prominent scholars signed and endorsed the contents of a statement entitled "A Secular Humanist Declaration." This was initially drafted by Paul Kurtz, editor of *The Humanist* magazine.[2]

Kurtz said he initiated the drafting of the document because fundamentalism had become a "vociferous critic of secular humanism." The fundamentalists, he said, "want to turn the clock back to the pre-modern world, to repeal the modern, scientific world."[3]

The fundamentalist concern to look to the past as the "golden age" is especially repugnant to Kurtz, because there is "no better substitute" than reason and science "for the cultivation of human intelligence." "We believe," he says, that "the scientific method, though imperfect, is still the most reliable way of understanding the world."[4] The reaction to secular humanism and the recent media attention it is getting is quite varied. It ranges all the way from the "ho-hum" attitude of theologian Martin E. Marty to those who argue that the moving force behind secular humanism is Satan himself.

Regardless, secular humanism as a particular kind of humanism has recently gained a new kind of prominence. For this reason it must be examined intelligently and critically by Christians. Recent critics of secular humanism have based their evaluation of this movement on the *Humanist Manifestoes I & II*. The more recently published "A Secular Humanist Declaration" is avowedly an extension of these documents and accepts the basic nontheistic evolutionary hypothesis set forth in them. In addition it affirms a commitment to ten points even though it claims these are not being set forth as a "dogma or creed." The best way to understand secular humanism is to let it speak for itself by summarizing and commenting on the ten points set forth in the Declaration.

Free Inquiry

Secular humanists insist on the inviolability of free inquiry and reject "any tyranny over the mind of men, any efforts by ecclesiastical, political, ideological, or social institutions to shackle free thought." The target for special concern in the document is the church, which is castigated for "bigotry" in its attempt to "censor inquiry" and "to impose orthodoxy on belief and values."[5]

There have been times, of course, in the history of the church when accusations of shackles, bigotry, and censorship were true. In A.D. 381, Emperor Theodosius

TEN THESES OF SECULAR HUMANISM

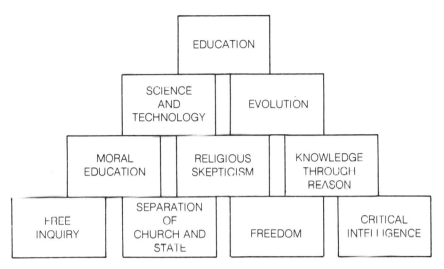

Figure 3

made Christianity the only legitimate religion of the Roman Empire; in the medieval period, popes ruled over nations and people with an iron hand, introducing the Inquisition and the Holy Crusades as means of "persuading" people of "truth." In more modern times we remember Calvin's Geneva experiment, the burning of witches in Salem, and the attempt of the Massachusetts Bay Colony to legislate religious uniformity.

Contemporary Christian humanism, however, also stands for free inquiry. It acknowledges the value of pluralism and seeks to establish its views by persuasion, not force, in the marketplace of ideas.

In this section of the Declaration, the authors affirm their commitment to "tolerate diversity of opinion" and to "respect the rights of individuals to express their belief." They declare that "truth is more likely to be discovered if the opportunity exists for the free exchange of opposing opinions."[6] Regrettably, secular humanists do not always practice what they preach. It is a matter of interest that the American Civil Liberties Union (ACLU) has gone to great lengths to ensure free speech for the Nazi party in this country, but has made strong efforts to put down the freedom of the new religious right to speak its mind. One could wish that secular humanists would grant religious groups the freedom they insist must be maintained for secular groups.

For the record, authentic Christian humanism believes in the triumph of truth, and it is more than willing to allow its point of view to compete in the agora of ideas. Competition is essential. Those religious persons or groups who try to *impose* their viewpoint on the public sector corrupt the true meaning of Christian humanism.

Separation of Church and State

It is obvious that the authors of "A Secular Humanist Declaration" believe that the church is altogether too willing to impose its viewpoint on society. "Clerical authorities," they say, "should not be permitted to legislate their parochial views." "The lessons of history are clear," the document states. "Wherever one religion or ideology is established and given a dominant position in the state, minority opinions are in jeopardy."[7]

Most Jewish thinkers would agree with the secularist concern to keep a particular religion from playing a dominant role in society. Although some Jews are supportive of the new religious right, most of them fear the potential of religious bigotry and a return to censorship of freedoms they suffered under other so-called Christian governments. The well-known Jewish novelist Chaim Potok put his finger on the issue in an interview with *Christianity Today* by advocating an a-religious society. For him, secularism has "no religious components." It is therefore a culture in which the Jew is free to engage in "sanctifying the behavior of Jews and of the world."[8]

But Christian humanists disagree with the modern interpreters of the separation of church and state who argue for the removal of religion as an influence in civil government. Christian humanists do not advocate a control of government by Christians. Nevertheless, because they believe Christianity is not a private matter, they seek to extend Christian influence into every aspect of the social order, including politics. For Christians, an *absolute* separation of church and state is impossible unless the church is suppressed and muzzled as much as it is behind the Iron Curtain.

Freedom

Secularists are against any kind of totalitarianism —religious or secular. For this reason, secular humanists attack communism as much as they castigate the church. The claim of Tim LaHaye, Jerry Falwell, and others that secular humanism is a tool of communism for the promotion of world socialism (or communism) is not supported by any statement in the Declaration.

"In communist countries," the Declaration states, "the power of the state is being used to impose an ideological doctrine on the society, without tolerating the expression of dissenting or heretical views."[9] In the opening words of the Declaration the authors declare they are "explicitly committed to democracy."

Freedom is also an ideal of authentic Christian humanism. God, having made man in his image, endowed him with freedom, even the freedom to rebel against his maker and to sin. Religious groups that seek to restrict personal freedom and to coerce all people to live according to their ethics fail to grasp the fact that God himself has given man the freedom to choose his own way. But this freedom includes the notion of accountability and responsibility. We cannot simply do whatever we please; we must accept the responsibility for the actions we take.

Critical Intelligence

The emphasis on critical intelligence is directed mainly toward moral values. Secular humanists reject the notion of moral absolutes that come from God and are passed down through the church. They argue that an adequate moral system for humanity need not depend upon "divine authority" or "religious commandments."

"Ethical judgments can be formulated independently of revealed judgments," the Declaration proclaims. The origin of ethics lies in "critical reason," a source of values that existed "long before religionists proclaimed their moral systems." "Morality that is not God-based," the authors say, "need not be anti-social, subjective, or promiscuous, nor need it lead to the breakdown of moral standards."[10]

Authentic Christian humanists acknowledge that all people are endowed with a certain sense of right and wrong. This conviction is rooted in the notion that God's laws are written into the hearts of man, and deep down in the consciousness of every person there is a witness to truth (see Rom. 2:14). Yet, Christian humanists argue for the need of divine revelation as an objective and ultimate standard against which to measure personal and societal behavior. When this standard is thrown away, there is no basis other than "human experience" to restrain human society from losing its sense of right and wrong. We can point to the current support for abortion, infanticide, euthanasia, genetic manipulation, and license in sexual matters as examples of what happens in a society that has no objective standard of ethics.

Moral Education

Because in their view there is no absolute system of morality, the secular humanists advocate a program of moral education in the public school system. Secular humanists claim they do not advocate a specific moral code but present "a *method* for the explanation and discovery of rational moral principles"[11] (emphasis added). This "method" is that of teaching children moral alternatives in order to encourage "moral awareness and the capacity for free choice." This, they argue, is the "duty of public education."

Authentic Christian humanism is in disagreement with secular humanism on several points in this matter. First, we believe it is highly questionable that moral choices can be neutral. How can a child, whose mind is immature, be exposed to "alternatives" and given free choice?

For example, the secular humanists, having no objective moral standards, may set heterosexual relationships alongside homosexual relationships as though both are equally valid lifestyles. Yet these same secular humanists regard it immoral to instruct children about religious matters. "We do not think it is moral to baptize infants, to confirm adolescents, or to impose a religious creed on young people before they are able to consent," the authors proclaim.[12] There seems to be a major contradiction here. The secular humanist wants to set the child up to accept moral relativism, but calls religious instruction of the young immoral!

Skepticism

Secular humanists are clear about their fundamental attitude toward religion: they are self-proclaimed skeptics. Although secular humanists claim they have no creed, clearly they consider the universe to be a dynamic scene of natural forces that are most effectively understood by scientific inquiry." For them, traditional views about God are "meaningless" and "tyrannically exploitive."[13]

It readily becomes clear that the "skepticism" of secular humanism is closer to zealous atheism. "We reject," the authors write, "the divinity of Jesus," the "idea that God has intervened miraculously in history or revealed himself." Rejecting God, secularists insist that "men and women are free and are responsible for their own destinies and that they cannot look toward some transcendent Being for salvation."[14]

Assertions such as these show the "total system" nature of secular humanism, to use a phrase suggested by Francis Schaeffer. Authentic Christian humanism comes from a completely opposite point of view, as has already been demonstrated. The two points of view represent a "clash of systems" at the foundational level of presuppositions.

Knowledge Through Reason

For the secular humanist, reason is the ultimate means of knowing truth. "We are committed to the uses of the rational methods of inquiry, logic, and evidence in developing knowledge and testing claims to truth," say the authors of the Declaration.[15]

Christian humanists are also committed to the use of the mind and the ability to reason. But there is a difference. The Christian acknowledges the mind as a gift from God to be used in understanding the world that God created. In fact, it was Christian humanism, with its emphasis on the mind and its affirmation of the Creation, that laid the groundwork for science. The geniuses whose discoveries and observations paved the way for modern science—men like Johannes Kepler, Galileo Galilei, and Sir Isaac Newton—all retained the theistic world-view inherited from the Middle Ages that the universe has a meaning and that it is possible to know what the meaning is and humanity's place in it. But gradually, during and after the seventeenth century, scholars began to divorce their scientific inquiry from a theistic world-view. The secularist differs from the Christian in that he makes the mind ultimate, freeing it from submission to the revelation that God has made in Scripture.

Autonomous reason, therefore, seeks to understand and interpret the world apart from its Creator. The Christian, using the same tools of reason and science, simply interprets the data of the earth in relationship to a commitment to its source. An example may be seen in the commitment Christians make to the origin of the universe through the divine activity of the Creator, refusing to set science in opposition to Creation.

Science and Technology

The secular humanist affirms faith in the god of Science and Technology. Science and Technology are the saviors of the world; they will solve all our problems. For secularists, the current environmental problems as well as the problems of hunger and poverty will someday be solved by science. Secularists reflect the spirit of Lewis Thomas, a scientist and the author of *The Lives of a Cell*, who wrote, "I take it as an article of faith that we humans are profoundly immature species, only now beginning the process of learning how to learn."[16] What he means is that man can and will solve the problems of humanity eventually.

Secularists are characterized by an underlying hope that applied science will someday turn the corner in solving the problems which humanity faces and thereby usher in the golden era. For this reason, the Declaration urges its readers to resist "unthinking efforts to limit technological or scientific advances."

Christian humanists do not reject the positive uses

of science and technology. Certainly science and technology have made significant strides in medicine, agriculture, communications and other areas which have benefited mankind. What Christian humanists reject is *faith* in science and technology—the naïve hope that science will eventually eradicate all human problems, including evil.

Evolution

Secular humanists are also committed to an atheistic theory of evolution. According to the Declaration, evolution has not yet "reached its final formulation," nor can it be said to be "an infallible principle of science." Nevertheless, the authors argue that evolutionary theory is "supported impressively by the findings of many sciences."[17]

Even though they admit to no "final proof" in the matter of evolution, the secularists take pains to single out the fundamentalist desire to teach scientific creationism in the classroom. According to the secularists, "This is a serious threat both to academic freedom and to the integrity of the educational process." They call it "a sham to make an article of religious faith as a scientific truth and to inflict that doctrine on the scientific curriculum." The teaching of creationism could have its place in the classroom, but should be taught in courses dealing with "religion and the history of ideas."[18] The response of fundamentalists is that evolution is a "theory" because it is not proven beyond a doubt and that the secular humanist agenda in teaching evolution goes beyond science into religion by its implication that evolution is nearly a scientific fact.

Education

The essential method to build a society that is humane and free is education. In the matter of education, secular humanists are particularly alarmed over the negative influence of television and the fact that it is replacing the schools as the major source of public information. They point out that in totalitarian societies the media serve "as the vehicle of propaganda and indoctrination," while in democratic societies the media often cater to "the lowest common denominator."[19]

A matter of special concern to the secularists is the fact that the media are "inordinately dominated by a religious bias." This observation is particularly interesting in light of Tim LaHaye's contention that the secularists have completely taken over the media centers of the West.

Nevertheless, the secularists claim that "the views of preachers, faith healers, and religious hucksters go largely unchallenged, and the secular outlook is not given an opportunity for a fair hearing." Therefore they call upon the secular humanists to "embark upon a long-term program of public education and enlightenment concerning the relevance of the secular outlook to the human condition."[20] Christians believe they have already succeeded in doing that.

In summary, let us think through the ten major points of secular humanism: free inquiry; separation of church and state; freedom; critical intelligence; evolution; moral educaiton; religious skepticism; knowledge through reason; science and technology; and education.

The most striking and recurring theme which runs through every point is that the church and Christianity are the enemy of the people and progress and that man himself has the capacity to save the world.

But *is* man his own savior? Or, are there some potential dangers within the secular humanist confidence in man and science that make the scenario of a world ruled by the secularist a frightening and dangerous spectacle?

POTENTIAL DANGERS OF SECULAR HUMANISM

It is a strange coincidence that the recent rise in religious emphasis is paralleled by a rise of secular humanism. According to the Gallup Poll of 1981, published under the title *Religion in America,* 93 percent of Americans have a religious preference. Of these, a full 70 percent belong to a church or synagogue. Nearly half of them attend services of worship regularly. Yet abortion, drugs, pornography, and moral permissiveness are on the rise. These trends demand an answer to the question, What happens to a free society when its major source of values is challenged and destroyed? Or, to put it another way—What are the potential dangers to society if secular humanism continues to influence the social order unchecked? There are, I believe, four dangers. They are destructive and irresponsible freedom; naïve utopianism that may introduce totalitarianism; moral chaos; and loss of human dignity.

Destructive and Irresponsible Freedom

By all accounts, Aleksandr Solzhenitsyn is a man whose experience under totalitarian government places him in a position of credibility to judge the West. In his famous Harvard speech in 1978 Solzhenitsyn warned against a "destructive and irresponsible freedom" that has been "granted boundless space." "Society," he said, "appears to have little defense against the abyss of human decadence."[21]

The point he was making—one with which the Christian humanist would agree—is that a distinction must be made between liberty and license. Someone once said, "Liberty stops where my nose begins." The issue between liberty and license is a bottom-line issue in the current differences of opinion between Christians and secular humanists in almost every aspect of morality.

For a Christian, freedom is restricted by its obligation to care for the needs of others. For this reason, Christians care about the rights of the unborn and want to restrict abortion; Christians care about the rights of children and seek to restrict pornographers and child molesters; Christians care about the moral development of their children and want to have something to say to those who write books and television scripts and produce movies; Christians care about their teen-agers and fear that the sanction of drugs and the freedom to obtain them will prove harmful to their development.

The secular humanists who also demonstrate a great deal of interest in these issues always seem to stand on the side of human freedom. They defend the right of the mother to abort her child; the right of the pornographer to promote and sell his smut; the right of homosexuals to teach their way of life in schools as a "neutral" option so students can make their own choices; and they campaign for the right to show X-rated movies, as well as the right to treat delicate sexual matters in a free and open way on TV, in the classroom, and in the theater. The danger of the secularist point of view is that it promotes a sick, narcissistic society in which no one thinks in terms of anything but "my" rights.

The well-known Christian humanist G. K. Chesterton once wrote, "The trouble when people stop believing in God is not that they thereafter believe in nothing; it is that they thereafter believe in anything."[22] In the case of the secular humanist, "anything" is a self-centered fulfillment to the neglect of human obligations. In the end, secular humanism has no basis from which to argue for caring for one another apart from a sentimental appeal to human experience and the value of altruism; yet even this has no authority behind it other than the consensus of those who agree it is good to "care for your neighbor."

Thus the first danger of secular humanism is that it undermines the basis on which a strong society is built, because it promotes a self-centered approach to life. Unrestricted freedom potentially leads to chaos and to the ruination of law and cultural norms.

Naïve Utopianism That May Introduce Totalitarianism

In the thinking of secular humanists, freedom is the basis for hope in the future. "If only man can be free, he will create the good society" is the fundamental thinking of utopianism.

The major flaw in naïve utopianism is its failure to take into account the evil inherent in man's nature. Solzhenitsyn describes the disintegration of the Western world as a "tilt of freedom in the direction of evil" which was born "out of a humanistic and benevolent concept according to which there is no evil inherent in human nature."[23]

This naïve view of man can be seen in the history of utopian literature. The theme is always that of man saving himself and introducing the perfect society. In his celebrated work *The Republic,* Plato argues that the ideal of a communal life can be achieved when the state is permitted to organize society in keeping with its own conception of justice. Thomas More argues in his well-known work *Utopia* for a society in which people live according to "virtue," a quality of goodness that characterizes all people. In the *New Atlantis,* Francis Bacon emphasizes the application of science for the creation of a good society. In the center of his ideal community there exists a house of science and technique, a laboratory, a bureau of planning, and a workshop. From this center will flow the development of a perfect society.

By the nineteenth century the concept emerged that an altruistic society would be based on some kind of collectivization. So, in Edward Bellamy's *Looking Backward*, the hope of the future was modeled on the notion that human motives will automatically adapt to the modifications of the environment. In the new society all human ills, anxieties, and struggles will be banished, providing the context in which the best of man will emerge. In the twentieth century the utopian dream of a controlled environment and an inherently good man looks more like the nightmare of George Orwell's *1984*. The scenario of a technological totalitarianism has been creeping up on Western man and now looms before us.

Unfortunately secular humanism has no ability to deal with the potential control of man by some sinister totalitarianism, because of its naïve view of the inherent goodness of man and its unqualified commitment to science and technology as the savior of the world. The fact is that when freedom goes wild and "every man does what is right in his own eyes" (as the Book of Judges puts it), a strong figure arises to produce order through totalitarian means. It happened in Germany in this century and, though for a different reason, more recently in Poland. The naïve opinion that "it can't happen here" is a dangerous attitude which will prevent people from turning things around before it happens. The Christian also believes in freedom, but it is a freedom to serve God and our neighbor, not a freedom to do whatever we want to do whenever we want to do it.

Moral Chaos

The notion that man is free from any higher force places man in the dilemma of having to determine what is right and wrong. In the West the notion that God defines the limits of human conduct has been the basis on which societal laws were established. Even though it is irrational and indefensible to view America as a "Christian" nation, the point can be made that our founders accepted the notion of a supreme being and viewed the moral heritage of Judaism and Christianity as foundational to the governance of society. But this consensus has been increasingly called into question in the rise of autonomous man. The question is, What are the dangers of a morality without divine sanction?

The first danger is moral chaos. If man himself is the final arbiter of moral rules by which society is governed, then men can change the rules as they see fit. But if it is true that our moral nature is fallen, as Christian humanism argues, then man's collective moral life will move toward the lowest common denominator. Is this not what Paul is saying in Romans 1 when he states that "God gave them over"? The implication is that when man removes the restraint of law, God allows the race to pursue their inclinations to the full. The danger of secular humanism is that, in its insistence on human autonomy and freedom, it may lead society over the brink. Were it not for God's common grace, society would affirm a moral chaos that would be its own ruination.

Paul Kurtz, a leading secular humanist, describes the moral libertarianism that the secular humanist advocates. "There is," he writes, "a more tolerant attitude toward sexual freedom and a demand that laws against abortion, birth control, and voluntary sterilization be repealed. There is a change in public attitudes towards pornography and obscenity, in increased acceptance of nudity on stage and in the cinema—especially where artistic values are involved—and in a conviction that society should not impose narrow standards of censorship. There is also a more liberal attitude toward the vagaries of sexuality."[24]

The argument of the Christian humanist against unbridled freedom is that when morality loses its foundation in divine law, there is no adequate means to keep the dam from breaking loose.

Loss of Human Dignity

The failure to have an adequate basis for human dignity opens the door to viewing human beings as worthwhile only if they are contributing members of society. The stands taken by the secular humanists concerning abortion and euthanasia demonstrate that secularists frequently demean the value of the life of the unborn and senile.

Eugene Diamond, professor of pediatrics at Loyola University in Chicago, speaking to a pro-life convention in St. Louis in October 1981, said the rise of the Nazis in Germany was accompanied by "a subtle shift in the attitude of physicians that there was such a thing as a life not worthy to live." According to Diamond, the present shift in the United States toward the demeaning of life is demonstrated in the procedures that have been developed to test the fetus for chromosomal disorders. These tests have "established a free-fire zone during which children with disorders can be killed." He added, "Genetics becomes religious dogma."

Diamond is equally concerned over the fact that life-saving operations are being withheld from children with Down's Syndrome. Frequently these children are denied food and water, and they die within two weeks from starvation. "We are substituting quality of life for the sanctity of life," Diamond said. "It is as though life is not life unless it is *la dolce vita.*"

This certainly seemed to be true in the celebrated case of the mother in Boston who, when she discovered that one of the two babies she was carrying had Down's Syndrome, ordered it to be killed through the heart with a needle. Coleman McCarthy, a Washington writer, observed in *Commentary,* "Life is sacred, everyone agrees, except when. . . . This list of 'exceptions' is a display of double standards. Either all of life is worth protecting—prenatal life included—or none is."

This is also the concern of June Goodfield in her book *Playing God.* "Man . . . can direct his own destiny," she writes. "Pick the good, specify the 'ideal' *Homo sapiens* and science will take us there."[25]

Tragically, the Supreme Court's ruling on abortions in 1973 has made American people think that abortion is not only legal, but ethical. If the Supreme Court, or human experience, or the consensus of the ruling elite is the source of values, then whatever they make legal will eventually become the accepted ethical norm.

The problem with secular humanism lies not only in the fact that it has no supreme reference point to make an appeal for ethical absolutes, but that it invariably makes man the final reference point for truth and morality. But man, says the Christian humanist, is by nature a sinful creature. This bent toward sin needs some kind of restraint external to man himself. Without it he may create the scenario described by Paul in Romans 1 or the vivid illustration of his inhumanity experienced in this century by the communist revolutions, the Nazi holocaust, and the abortion of unwanted children. The danger of secular humanism is that it contains no internal conviction or means to restrain the madman who would like to control human destiny.

In summary, there are several basic points to keep in mind about secular humanism.

• Secular humanism belongs to the nontheistic family of humanism.

• A special feature of secular humanism is its atheistic fervor.

• The "Secular Humanist Declaration" singles out the church and Christianity as the major enemies of man and progress.

- Secular humanism is a threat to society because it has no ultimate basis for morality and the restraint of freedom.

It is impossible to give a statistical measurement of how pervasive secular humanism is within Western society. According to Tim LaHaye, "They [secular humanists] control everything—the mass media, government, and even the Supreme Court." But in an article entitled "The Humanist Phantom," Charles Krauthammer says, "It remains an enthusiastic, slightly utopian, and doggedly atheistic forum for a small group of believers."

Regardless, it appears that the clash of systems between Christianity and secular humanism is building. The following chapters demonstrate where the battle lines have been drawn in the moral, social, educational, and political arenas.

II

The Clash
of Systems

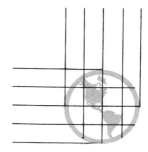

4

The Playboy Mentality

"They have labeled the Moral Majority the extreme right because we speak out against extreme wrong," Jerry Falwell says of his critics. In one of his earliest letters, Falwell wrote:

Just look at what's happening here in America:
- Homosexual teachers have invaded the classrooms, and the pulpits of our churches.
- Smut peddlers sell their pornographic books under the protection of the U.S. Constitution!
- And X-rated movies are allowed in almost every community because there is no legal definition of obscenity.
- Meanwhile, right in our own homes the television screen is full of R-rated movies and sex and violence.
- Believe it or not, we are the first civilized nation in history to legalize abortion — in the late months of pregnancy! Murder!

The reaction to Falwell's letter and suggested program of reform was immediate. In an undated letter issued by the American Humanist Association, it was stated that the legislation proposed in these matters "are contrary to *your* interests as an American with unique and alternative views. Such programs, if effected, would control education, our state and federal laws, and our freedoms—and this may be just the beginning."

"Their kind of 'patriotism' violates every principle of liberty that underlies the American system of government," wrote Norman Doren, the President of the American Civil Liberties Union. In another letter, Nor-

man Lear, the producer of "Mary Hartman, Mary
Hartman" and other TV situation comedies, quotes
Edward Erickson as stating, "The corrupters of youth
and the nation come more from the purveyors of the
obscenity of religious malice, the obscenity of social
strife disguised as the struggle of decency, of reaction
parading as a guardian of the American home, of fas-
cism masquerading as Christianity. This is the ultimate obscenity, the spiritual pornography of debased
religiosity."

The issue between Christian humanism and secular humanism comes down to freedom versus order.
How free ought a society to be? Should it tolerate an
open and permissive morality? Is a homosexual lifestyle acceptable? Should pornographers be allowed to
sell their goods in the open?

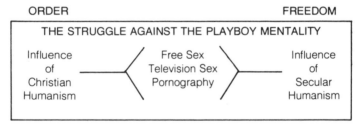

Figure 4

FREE SEX

In a recent television interview, Hugh Hefner, the
founder of *Playboy* magazine and Playboy Enterprises,
was asked, "What do you believe is your greatest
achievement in life?" Without hesitation Hefner said, "I
feel fulfilled in life because I have played a major role in
the sexual revolution of our time. As a result of my work
and example, I have helped people become more com-

fortable with sexual freedom and, in that way, I've contributed to the enrichment of life" (paraphrased). Not everyone agrees that free sex is for the enrichment of life. This is particularly true of the Chicago Counter-Playboy Movement, which meets annually in front of the Chicago-based Playboy center to protest the Playboy mentality. Hundreds have gathered in protest against *Playboy*. They have issued a Chicago Statement and hope at a future time to fill Wrigley Field with thousands of people who will let it be known that the Playboy mentality is unacceptable.

Richard Halverson, the chaplain of the U.S. Senate, has written, "The Chicago Statement is timely and relevant. I commend it for the thoughtful consideration of every concerned American. It represents profound insight into the present condition of our national life."

A former Playboy bunny, Brenda Miller—now a Christian—writes, "I became morally bankrupt and was a witness to the devastation it brought to many other lives."[1]

After the Counter-Playboy Movement's protest banquet in 1981, Brad Carl, a Washington artist and art dealer, was asked, "Why pick on Playboy?" Carl answered, "Playboy symbolizes the acceptance we have given to treating women as commercial sexual commodities. . . . Hefner has packaged sleazy sex with Madison Avenue glamour . . . America gets the idea that the Playboy philosophy is acceptable without ever really thinking it through."[2]

Thinking it through and changing America's attitude toward the Playboy mentality is the goal of the Chicago Statement group. There is, they insist, an "obvious correlation between the lifestyle promoted therein and the epidemic social sickness we see today. Increasing numbers of teen-age pregnancies, abortions, fatherless children, divorces, and epidemic venereal disease have a direct correlation to the lifestyles promoted in these magazines."[3]

For this reason Catholics, mainline congregations from Episcopal, Methodist, Presbyterian, and Lutheran churches, and evangelicals gather annually to let their witness be heard against the corrupting influence of the Playboy mentality. "It took Playboy Enterprises many years of hard work to make pornography acceptable in America's family marketplace. It will take us a few years of prayer and hard work to make a significant response to that influence and to turn things around."[4]

Protest is a legitimate and perhaps highly effective way for Christians to raise their voices for morality in society. It is a peaceful, noncoercive, and non-manipulative form of witness.

TELEVISION SEX

Christians are becoming increasingly aware of the way in which television promotes the Playboy mentality. "There is a revolution under way," wrote Charles Reich in his book *The Greening of America*. "It is now spreading with amazing rapidity, and already our laws, institutions, and social structure are changing in consequence."[5]

One of the institutions in this country that reflects the secularist revolution is the television industry. What passes today for art and entertainment would have been considered "trash" and pornography twenty years ago.

The confrontation between Christian values and a secularist viewpoint is occurring through the leadership of the Reverend Donald E. Wildmon, chairman of the Coalition for Better Television. In February 1980, Wildmon called for a national boycott of products from the sponsors of programs containing explicit sexuality, violence, and profanity. Ruth Dolan, the director of the

Coalition in Denver, Colorado, voiced the concern of its members when she said, "Television has simply gone too far in allowing the display of sex and violence."[6] Apparently Ruth Dolan is not alone in this conviction. A recent poll revealed that 60 percent of the Americans surveyed agreed that "television and other media in this country reflect a permissive and immoral set of values which are bad for this country." Even though Proctor and Gamble agreed to withdraw its sponsorship from fifty programs considered objectionable, it appears that other advertisers are not going to follow their lead. So we can expect an increase of sex on the television screen. This judgment seems to have been confirmed in a recent debate between Gene Nater, the senior vice-president of CBS, and Donald Wildmon. Nater said, "Mister Wildmon is a minister and has a stated set of values. I am a broadcaster and do not."[7]

The recent decision of NBC to produce a major mini-series from the book *Princess Daisy* "probably makes a confrontation inevitable," according to Wildmon. The theme of this novel by Judith Krantz is promiscuity and adultery. It features an episode in which a thirty-two-year-old woman seduces a fourteen-year-old child; it contains an affair between a brother and sister; and a sexual relationship between two women. Prime-time soap operas such as "Falcon Crest," "Dallas," and "Dynasty" win consistently high ratings. In March 1982, the "inevitable" apparently happened: Wildmon called for a boycott of NBC programming.

Studies have found that teen-agers are especially attracted to programs with sexual themes. A recent study, headed by Bradley Greenburg and published in the University of Pennsylvania *Journal of Communication*, concludes that 94 percent of inferred sexual relationships on television do not involve married couples. Greenburg observed that "soap operas may be a major force in the transmission of values and life-styles and sexual information to young viewers."[8]

According to a report in *America* (June 13, 1981), the situation could get worse. The advent and growth of cable television has opened up new outlets for pornography. "Adult" networks such as *Escapade, Private Screenings,* and *Penthouse* are seeking to obtain franchise operations which will channel adult movies into subscribing homes. "We may find our homes knee-deep in 'adult' garbage," writes the author in a concluding statement in the *America* report.

There is no easy solution to the rise of morally permissive television programing. The protest of the Christian public is certainly a legitimate and perhaps effective way to counteract it. In addition, the church must become more clear about the application of its values to societal issues. These issues must be addressed through preaching and teaching, with an emphasis on the responsibility of Christian families to control the television sets in their own homes.

PORNOGRAPHY

The spread and availability of pornography contributes significantly to the moral permissiveness of our society. Cal Thomas, the vice-president of communications of the Moral Majority, recently announced that the organization will mount an anti-pornography campaign using legal, economic, and political pressure to stop pornographic traffic. "The hard statistics show that where these businesses [that sell pornography] are allowed to proliferate, the tax base is eroded, the crime rate increases," Thomas says.[9]

Is pornography a matter of personal taste, or does it indeed lead to crimes of violence? Observers believe that public apathy regarding pornography is rooted in the belief that it is a "victimless crime." But Adelaide Nimitz, who regularly pickets a twenty-four-hour adult bookstore in California, claims that "the sex shop traffic brings in prostitutes, and they bring in the drug traffic. Then people burglarize our homes to get money for dope."[10]

But it is not easy to legislate against pornography, because of the First Amendment that guarantees freedom. In Mount Ephraim, New Jersey, for example, an adult bookstore that features nude dancing was taken to court. The court upheld the right of the bookstore to continue its live entertainment on the basis of the First Amendment. Nevertheless, it was determined that Mount Ephraim could establish a zoning law that prohibits sleazy exhibitions and through such a law terminate the nude dancing. In the end, it was not the issue of nudity that brought a stop to the dancing, but the breaking of a zoning law.[11]

Nevertheless, the $4 billion pornography business is very difficult to restrain. A recent *U.S. News & World Report* account suggests that "adult entertainment no longer is confined to big city porno districts. The market is moving to better neighborhoods—and even into the family home."[12]

One way by which pornography is moving into the home is through the fairly recent marketing of video cassettes. More than one million Americans own video-cassettes equipment. Dealers in X-rated movies, which sell from $80 to $150, report that sales are rising. Barry Maddox, who owns a video-tape store in Washington, D.C., says, "Customers demand the X-rated, and we sell them because we aren't going to send our customers somewhere else." Bruce Taylor, a lawyer in Cleveland, comments, "People are bringing home the kind of movies people used to go to jail for."[13]

The spread of pornography is difficult to stop. Those who are against pornography "complain about vague laws, weak penalties, inadequate police efforts and lagging public interest," writes Jeanne Thornton in *U.S. News & World Report.*[14]

Nevertheless, Christians are becoming increasingly vocal. An interdenominational group of Christians in Dallas recently issued the "Dallas Statement" that decries the spread of pornography: "We have watched while young children have been enslaved and sold as sexual merchandise to fuel the pornography industry. We are appalled that the entertainment media with its emphasis on casual promiscuity has become a major tool for the degradation of true human sexuality." The writers of the document urge Christians to break their silence and to reaffirm scriptural "principles which promote human dignity, protect our children from sexual exploitation, and provide healthy roles for the expression of human sexuality."

The Playboy mentality has also engendered a rise in drugs, explicit sexual language in contemporary music, increased consumption of alcohol, and homosexuality as an alternative lifestyle.

Authorities estimate that nearly $45 billion worth of drugs were sold illegally in the United States in 1978. "Not only is the United States the most pervasive drug-abusing nation in history," says Congressman Lester Wolff, chairman of the House of Representatives Select Committee on Narcotics Abuse and Control, "but drug abuse among our children has risen in the past two years, from epidemic to pandemic proportions."[15]

Furthermore, children listen to explicit sexual language and sounds in much of the rock and "Top 40" music. Bob Larson, a former rock performer, says in his book *Rock,* "Nothing is left to the imagination. Every intimate detail pertaining to the physical aspect of sex is thoroughly explained to the teen-age mind."[16]

What can Christians do about the rise of pornography, the spread of drugs, and explicitly sexual language in music? The fact is that there is very little the church can do directly to stem the tide of pornography. The regulation and control of these immoral industries are under the jurisdiction of the government, and, for this reason, lie beyond the immediate reach of the Christian.

Nevertheless, there are indirect ways Christians can make an impact on the pornography trade. At the very least, we should not support these immoral businesses by buying any of their products; we can also support groups that attempt to raise the level of awareness by pointing to the results of these evils; we can also vote on legislation that would restrict the proliferation of pornography through stricter zoning laws as well as laws having to do with the public display of lewd material.

On the other hand, we must avoid making this issue or similar issues the primary focus of the church. The church is not a legislating body, and thus it should avoid the temptation to change society through political power lest it become obsessed with its own power and deluded into thinking it can Christianize society through law.

CONCLUSION

Here is a summary of the basic issues before us:

- Our society is characterized by a Playboy mentality.

- Many television programs are characterized by the promotion of free and illicit sex.

- Easy access to pornography contributes significantly to moral permissiveness.

There can be no doubt that the Playboy mentality has made its impact on our society, plunging it toward moral chaos. This leads us to ask, "What lies at the bottom of the Playboy mentality?" It is, we answer, *the insatiable desire to be free—free from moral restraint,*

*free to pursue personal momentary pleasure as an
end in itself.*

But where is the church while all this goes on? If
we merely condemn or sit idly by while society becomes
even more permissive, we fail to apply the gospel to all
of life.

The church must turn away from "hate cam-
paigns" or attempts to solve the problems of society
through censorship. It must offer a living alternative
and be a loving society within the society. It must offer
healing and forgiveness to sinners and open its doors
to those who are needy and oppressed. It must seek to
meet the needs of real people where they are and offer
an alternative to the morally debilitating attractions of
society.

There is no easy or quick solution to these issues.
It will take a long time for the church to recover its
influence, because it has been silent too long, and secularism has been allowed to permeate our society and
introduce a revolution toward temporary freedom,
away from order and stability.

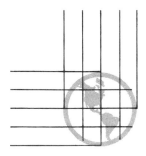

5

The Violent Society

"The devil made me do it," a phrase popularized in a comedy TV show several years ago, has become a household phrase on the lips of many people who want to make a joke out of their escapades. For Superior Court Judge Robert Callahan in Danbury, Connecticut, it is hardly a joke. It's a legal problem. A young man in his court, having killed a friend in a quarrel, claimed in his defense that he was possessed by the devil.

Christian humanism recognizes that society is not what it ought to be, because of the Fall. Paul speaks of the Christian's former life as one in which "you followed the ways of this world and of the ruler of the kingdom of the air, the spirit who is now at work in those who are disobedient" (Eph. 2:2). The phrase "ruler of the kingdom" is a reference to obedience to the powers of evil. Paul lists some of these powers for the Galatian Christians: "Sexual immorality, impurity and debauchery; idolatry and witchcraft; hatred, discord, jealousy, fits of rage, selfish ambition, dissensions, factions and envy; drunkenness, orgies, and the like" (Gal. 5:19–21).

Because individual persons are in the grip of evil, the corporate culture they create is an extension of themselves, a mirror that images the depth to which human depravity can sink. But Christians are called to live by a different power—the power of the Holy Spirit, which Paul describes as the power that produces "love, joy, peace, patience, kindness, goodness, faithfulness, gentleness and self-control" (Gal. 5:22–23). Christian activity in society should therefore produce different results. The unfolding of culture by Christians should produce a corporate extension of the Christian person.

Unfortunately it isn't that simple. The fact is that the unconverted are not so far fallen that they cannot produce good works, and the converted are not so perfected that they don't sin. This is due on the one hand to the common grace of God, which is a restraint against evil for the unbeliever; and to sanctification, on the other hand, which is the process of the believer's growing toward a fulfillment of the ideal.

Consequently the tension between what is and what ought to be is expressed within society itself in the contest with evil. Here the antithesis between the Christian and the secularist is not always clear. Sometimes the secularist, because of common grace, is as equally concerned about societal issues as is the Christian. And sometimes the Christian is found supporting matters like war and capital punishment that are expressions of violence.

This chapter will focus on violence as it expresses itself in many facets of society such as war, television, the family and child abuse, and abortion.

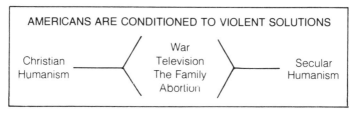

Figure 5

NUCLEAR WAR

It is becoming increasingly clear that nuclear war is an outrage against humanity. But the arguments that the secularists offer against nuclear war are rather thin as opposed to those that can be offered by the Christian. The secularist can speak about the value of human life, yet fail to have an ultimate reason why life is valuable. The secularist can speak about caring for the environment, but fail to offer a convincing reason why the environment is so important.

Christian humanism is against war and the violence it produces, because God is the Creator of the world and mankind is made in his image. To destroy man and the Creation is an attack upon God's creative work and an affront to God himself.

"War is the work of man. War is destruction of human life. War is death," said Pope John Paul II at the Hiroshima Peace Memorial on February 25, 1981. He called war "one of humanity's sad achievements" and called upon people around the world "to act in harmony with the demands of peace rather than out of narrow self-interest." He called on governments and the heads of state around the world to "work untiringly for disarmament and the banishing of all nuclear weapons; let us replace violence and hate with confidence and caring."[1]

Billy Graham, the leading spokesman for evangelical Christianity, made the same plea in an interview with *Sojourners* magazine in August 1979. Among other things, he said, "I believe that the Christian especially has a responsibility to work for peace in our world. Christians may well find themselves working and agreeing with non-believers on an issue like peace. *But our motives will not be identical*" (emphasis added).

Recently Christians have gathered to discuss ways in which the church and parachurch groups could support peace. One group, the Covenant Peace Making Program, has issued a "World Peace Pledge" which simply states, "In light of my faith, I am prepared to live without nuclear weapons in my country." Other groups have joined together in the preparation of the "New Abolitionist Covenant" in which they state, "We have become convinced that Jesus' call to be peacemakers urgently needs to be renewed in the churches and made specific by a commitment to abolish nuclear weapons and to find a new basis of national security."

Christians, however, are divided over the issue. For the most part, members of the religious right support military buildup as a way of preserving peace. For them, nuclear disarmament would put America in a position of weakness and vulnerability to an attack and takeover by the Russians. There are secularists who agree with this position on the same political grounds.

Nevertheless, Christians are becoming increasingly aware that the calling of the church is to peacemaking. A "hawkish" attitude seems to contradict the direct teachings of Jesus and is hardly compatible with the peacemaking role of the church in the world. In the end, it is God who is in control of history, and the church is to trust in His providence over the world, rather than military might.

TELEVISION VIOLENCE

The presence of violence in our homes has become increasingly evident since television carried the war of Vietnam into the privacy of our living room. The world ate dinner or snacked as they watched people having their heads shot off, villages being destroyed, and children wandering the streets dazed, homeless, and hungry. Today the violence on the tube is less likely to be news-related: it runs through the storyline of cops and robbers programs.

Christians have taken up arms against this and other kinds of television violence because of their conviction that there is a direct relationship between violence on television and the increase of violence in our country. "We have come to a unanimous conclusion that there is a causal relationship between television violence and real-life violence," David Pearl said in a report for the National Institute of Mental Health.

In his testimony before the congressional hearings on television violence, Thomas Radecki said that 25 to 50 percent of the violence in our society is coming from the culture of violence being taught by our entertainment media, most strongly by the television and movie industries. This estimate is based on solid research findings."[2]

According to Radecki, a psychiatrist who heads up the National Coalition on Television Violence, the showing of The Deer Hunter, an Academy Award-winning movie on the war in Vietnam, has produced twenty-five documented cases of people shooting themselves. (Twenty-two have died.) Radecki has tried in vain to persuade television producers to keep the film off the air, but has received no positive response. "These guys are in it for the money," said Radecki. "Human life doesn't matter."[3] According to an article in Reader's Digest, a child has witnessed 18,000 television murders by the time he is eighteen years old. Could it be that we are becoming callous to violence?

Both Christians and non-Christians are responding to TV violence by demanding less violent television programing. The National Coalition on Television Violence includes both Christian and non-Christian people; the Coalition for Better Television, directed by the Reverend Donald Wildmon, draws Christian people together to oppose and boycott sponsors, if necessary, to halt the tide of violence. Christian people need to seize leadership in this matter and restrict the watching of television violence in their own homes. Children should not have unrestricted access to television.

FAMILY VIOLENCE

In recent years the breakdown of the family has subjected its victims to a *psychological violence.*

"Divorces nearly tripple in 20 years" exclaimed a headline in the June 22, 1981 issue of *U.S. News & World Report* magazine. In 1979 there were 1,181,000 divorces, a 4.5 percent rise over 1978, and they left more than 1.2 million youngsters under the age of 18 years of age with divorced parents.

"We asked for it," Meg Greenfield writes in a *Newsweek* column. "By 'we' I mean that mild, moderate, liberalish majority that has been roosting near the center of the nation's politics for years." We have, she says, "refused to view practically any indecency, outrage or pathological assault on our sense of rightness in any way except as a civil-liberties problem— protecting the abstract right of the sickos to come to dinner."[4]

The problem relates to the issue of freedom of responsibility. In the secular society, spawned by the loss of belief in a God to whom we are accountable, it has become fashionable for modern man to be free—free from covenantal agreements, free from the responsibility to raise children, free to pursue his own selfish desires. The result is a psychological violence that tears at the hearts of those victimized by divorce, especially the children.

How can we counteract this increase in the breakdown of the family? Recently a White House Family Conference agreed on "the vital need for family life education, and that government at all levels should assist the public and private sectors by providing appropriate courses for children and parents."[5] But who put government in control of the home? The fact is that government is not qualified to pontificate on the home.

Here is an opportunity for the church to make a significant contribution to society. New parachurch movements such as *Marriage Encounter* and an emphasis on marriage and family counseling emerging recently in our seminaries across this country are means of offering leadership in the vital matter of the home and family living.

But a two-pronged approach is needed. On the one hand, the church needs to be more sensitive to the needs of divorced parents and children. It needs to be more accepting, to find ways to offer love, comfort, and support to those who have suffered the violence of a broken home. On the other hand, it needs to develop strategies to teach and encourage people to accept the obligation of marriage and to remain married whenever possible. Moral permissiveness and the failure to uphold standards of fidelity and responsibility on the part of those secularists who advocate "finding yourself" with little or no regard for the consequences of selfish behavior need to be counteracted by the development of the clear and forthright teaching and standards of the church in this matter.

At a recent meeting of the National Council of Churches in Cleveland, noted ethicist Max Stackhouse of Andover Newton Theological Seminary in Massachusetts, whipped member churches for not addressing family problems. "The family is in enough trouble today," he said, "that to encourage, by word or example, that kind of promiscuity which breaks fidelity, to praise models of open marriage, to fail to reconstruct a vision of the Christian family at a time when older versions have been shown to be adequate, is simply to abandon our ethical anchors and drift with the tide of indulgence."[6]

There is another problem within the family that points to the increasing state of violence in our society. This is the matter of child abuse. In the 1970s, 50,000 children died of child abuse and another 30,000 were permanently damaged. According to recent statistics,

"One out of every ten children will end up spending time in a mental hospital. One out of fifteen will be an alcoholic. One out of nine will be in trouble with the law before the age of eighteen."[7] In 1966 the Department of Children and Family Services in Illinois had 483 referrals for child abuse. Ten years later the number jumped to 6,748, and more than 8,000 cases were reported in 1978.

Ruth Born, program specialist for the Children's Bureau of the U.S. Department of Health, Education and Welfare office in Chicago, said, "Somebody needs to say, straightout, what we all avoid saying: It is that the statistics on abuse and neglect mean that nobody cares."[8] Carol Zientek, probation officer for the Educational Advocacy, Juvenile Court of Cook County, Illinois, observed, "Many people disagree with the philosophy of the Moonies, but what have they given young people but a purpose in life? Our traditional religions seem to have drifted away from that: children are growing into adults with no purpose."[9]

Here again is where an authentic Christian humanism must say no to society. If we truly believe that children also are made in the image of God, then our efforts to raise them with a sense of self-worth, a sense of responsible duty, and a purpose in life ought to be doubled. The Christian Church has an obligation to go beyond the call to "conversion." It must educate families toward the responsibility and obligation of being Christian families.

But most parents—Christian and non-Christian alike—do not know how to parent. Therefore we tend to parent as we were parented—repeating the mistakes that were imposed on us by our parents. If children in the home are to be nurtured for the purpose of growing into their full potential as human beings, the church will have to address this problem both through educating its present families and through a reaching out to homes where children are neglected or battered to offer help where it is needed. Statistics show that there is a definite correlation between abused children, juvenile crime, and adult violence. If the church is to make an impact on society, it must start on the grass-roots level—in the home and with the children.

For example, Parents Anonymous is a church-related group that has recently emerged to help parents cope with the problems that lead to child abuse. Mark Dalebroux, a volunteer for the Mennonite Central Committee and director of Parents Anonymous in Georgia, says, "The actions of a child-abusing parent are not condoned, but they are understandable." The groups meet weekly for about two and one-half hours. Dalebroux says, "The groups are for the parents and run by the parents." They seek both to treat and to prevent child abuse by discussing common problems and ways to improve parenting skills. An authentic Christian humanism affirms this as a vital expression of the work of the church.[10]

ABORTION

The most heinous expression of violence in this country is found in the practice of abortion.

One of the gravest consequences of sin is the acceptance of violence as a means of solving problems. Ever since Cain killed his brother Abel, the history of human relationships has been marred by violence. Even the church in its Inquisition, holy wars, religious wars of the sixteenth century, and witch burnings has on occasion—and to its shame—resorted to violence as a way of solving a social problem. Our forefathers established a foothold in this country through the violent treatment of the Indians; America was founded in a bloody revolution and later fought a civil war over slavery. Other examples of American violence include the Mexican War; the Spanish-American War; the subjection of the American Indian on the western frontier; and the more recent war in Vietnam. So it is not completely out of character with this country in general, and secularism in particular, to solve the problem of unwanted pregnancies through violence.

In an article, *What are the Rights of the Unborns?* Coleman McCarthy pleads with the American society to find a nonviolent alternative to abortion. He believes that by abandoning the search for nonviolent choices, this society "sanctions the political and social system that has made it acceptable for the nation to rely on violent solutions."

It is difficult to deny that abortion is a "violent solution." In an abortion by Caesarean section, babies that are breathing and sometimes crying are frequently dropped in a bucket and left to die. In a salt-poisoning abortion which occurs after sixteen weeks, a long needle is inserted through the mother's abdomen into the sac and a solution of concentrated salt is injected into it. The baby breathes in and swallows the salt and is poisoned as a result. It takes more than an hour to kill a baby by this method—a method that also burns off the outer layer of the baby's skin. A D&C can be performed between seven and twelve weeks. In this method a sharp knife is inserted through the vagina into the uterus where the body is cut into pieces and the placenta is cut from the inside walls of the uterus. Before ten weeks, the suction method can be used: a powerful suction tube is inserted into the uterus and the body of the developing baby and its placenta are sucked into a jar. Often the bodily parts of the baby are visible.

Frank Holman, a medical doctor from Belleville, Illinois, reminds us of the events in Germany that led to the slaughter of more than six million Jews. "First, it practiced abortion on demand," he writes. "Then came 'euthanasia' to free the taxpayers of the burden of providing care to the mentally and physically handicapped. The moral climate which such ethics and practices generated was finally culminated by extermination camps for others who were 'less than human,' i.e., non-Aryans, political prisoners, and any no longer useful to society."[11]

If the church, which believes in the dignity of humanity because all persons are made in the image of God, will not uphold justice for the unborn, who will?

CONCLUSION

Here is a summary of the issues before us:

- Our society is characterized by a bent toward solving problems through violence.

- Nuclear war is the ultimate violence in a society unwilling to settle its differences through peaceful negotiations.

- Television violence has made the average American indifferent to the shock of destruction and death.

- The breakdown of the family has created a new terror—psychological violence that stalks the hearts and minds of its victims.

- Abortion is the most heinous and despicable violence practiced in this country against innocent human life.

These are five of a number of issues in society that raise the issue of violence against human beings. It is the conviction of an authentic Christian humanism that all life is of value. War, the effects of television, the family and child abuse, and abortion are issues that deal with the sanctity of human life. The American Civil Liberties Union may support the freedom of moral permissiveness which increases the divorce rate; it may support those who scream "censorship" when television violence is called into question; it may advocate the "right" of the mother over her own womb.

Christian humanism cannot support these expressions of violence. The voice of the church and the Christian must be heard in these matters. Yet the church must avoid political power and control as the way of achieving its end. The church as an institution may speak out against violence, it must teach its members Christian values, it should offer a community of support for its activists. But it must not go for the simplistic solution of political power. Rather, it needs to dig in for the long term—for the rebuilding of society through the inculcation of Christian values that are carried into various vocations through individual Christians.

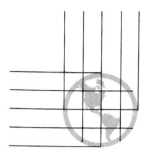

6

The Schoolroom Nightmare

"Their [secular humanists'] success in our public schools are well documented," Tim LaHaye writes. "Because of them, prayer, Bible reading, Bible study, released time classes, Easter, and Christmas celebrations have been eliminated."[1]

Furthermore, LaHaye and other leaders of the religious right would agree with the economist, Milton Friedman, that public schools are "an island of socialism in a free-market sea."[2] Some would even agree with Gordon Drake of the Christian Crusade that the National Education Association has created a school system in which "our children are being indoctrinated for a new collectivist world government."

Terrell H. Bell, the secretary of the U.S. Department of Education under President Reagan, intends to remove federal control from the schools and give control back to the states where he believes it belongs. "We must go back," he claims, "to the 10th Amendment of the Constitution to realize that in their wisdom our founding fathers delegated the responsibility for education to the states." Accordingly, Bell claims, the president's decision to reduce federal spending and intervention in education is to "free them from federal domination and possible ultimate control."[3]

The attempt to reduce direct government control of public education will be hailed as a positive development by right-wing and more moderate Christians. The Association for Public Justice, a Christian organization, observed that "a truly just government must encourage, protect and make room for the development and expression of the cultural freedom of individuals, groups and institutions in our society. This task is one of the primary responsibilities of our government."[4] This principle of "cultural freedom for individuals" opposes any attempt by the government to "create a homogeneous mass of citizens or a non-differentiated society."[5] It is precisely a uniform society that Christians fear. And the channel through which this could most conceivably occur is education. There are four areas in which this battle between secularists and Christians is now being waged: values clarification; sex education; the creation/evolution controversy; prayer and the observance of religious holidays in public schools.

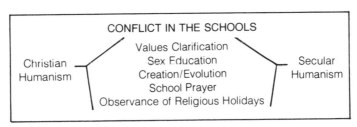

Figure 6

VALUES CLARIFICATION

One of the marks of Christian humanism is its strong belief in values. Christianity obviously is *not* a value-free point of view. The New Testament clearly teaches that the Christian convert is to "put off" the old man and "put on" the new man. This is a description of shedding one set of values to replace it with another.

More recently the issue of value training has become a predominant concern of educators. Timothy I. Crater, a pastor, wrote in *Christianity Today*, "The philosophy of education has undergone a fundamental change. Educators now perceive their job to be the complete 'resocialization' of the child—the complete reshaping of his values, beliefs and morals."[6]

This shift toward moral education, or what some have called "values clarification," was initiated in England in 1967 with the publication of Wilson, Williams, and Sugarman's *Introduction to Moral Education* and in the United States with Raths, Harmin, and Simon's *Values and Teaching* in 1966. The research of Lawrence Kohlberg on cognitive development, especially his book *The Philosophy of Moral Development*, and the seminar conducted by the Howard University Center for Moral Education, have helped this movement to gain rapid attention among American educators.

The purpose of values clarification is to assist young students, through small-group exercises and discussions, to come to terms with their own personal values and to formulate basic beliefs that will help them confront difficult choices. It has met both strong opposition and strong support, and it is increasingly becoming a battleground between Christians and secularists.

In Craig, Colorado, for example, a group of concerned parents has organized CARE (Concerned Adults Reviewing Education). Nearly five hundred parents signed a petition expressing fear "that many sessions conflict with religious beliefs taught at home, that respect for parental authority is subtly undermined through probing questions, and that the use of the program conflicts with the separation of church and state because it is humanistically oriented."[7]

One of the exercises in the course asks the students to answer, "What did your parents make you do yesterday that you did not want to do?" Mrs. Larry Naylor, whose husband heads CARE, said the courses "advocate situation ethics and teach a child to choose freely from all the alternatives, disregarding what the parents teach."[8]

Supporters of values clarification insist that the issue is indoctrination versus personal choice. For them the direct inculcation of adult values (such as the notion of the Ten Commandments and religious absolutes) is an outmoded method of education. Teaching values through rules and punishments or through instilling a fear of authority is ultimately ineffective, because values cannot be made personal by external pressure. On the other hand, Christians argue that because values cannot be neutral, posing questions that allow any answer to be correct produces an unhealthy relativism.

Values clarification will more than likely become increasingly prevalent in our schools as long as the Federal government controls education. Christians have several choices. One choice is to enroll their children in private Christian schools. Another is for Christian teachers in public education to deal with the subject in such a way that the Christian view of moral absolutes is given a fair hearing. Also, Christians can become involved in the discipline of moral development and help shape the textbooks that are being written.

In the final analysis, however, Christian moral education belongs in the church and the home. We need a cadre of people who are sensitive to the science of the moral development of the child to produce written material and training workshops in the church for teachers and parents. Christians have not been adequately attuned to these problems and have assumed too much in the moral development of their child, unthinkingly allowing them to be formed by forces outside the church and home. This is a pluralistic society, not a Christian nation. We can no more "force" our point of view on public education than can the secularists. But we can and we should compete in the marketplace of ideas and seek to express our viewpoint in those ways that are legitimately available to us in a democracy.

Sex Education

"Nearly half the nation's 15-to-19-year-old girls have had premarital sex—and the number is climbing," reports *Newsweek*.[9] Teen-age sex is touted everywhere as something to be desired, to be enjoyed, and to be pursued for personal fulfillment. The media are full of alluring sexual advertisements like those of the Jordache Jeans Company, in which teen-agers are suggestively portrayed half-nude.

Teen music, whether it be country western or rock, blares, "Take your time (Do it right)," "Do that to me one more time," and "Let's get physical." Movies like the soft porn of *Blue Lagoon* assert that teen sex is appropriate and a thing to be desired. Yet, according to one estimate, only 10 percent of American teen-agers have ever adequately studied the subject of sex.

For this reason, sex education is rapidly becoming a part of the public school curriculum—a development that has created heated debate. A *Glamour* survey published in June 1981 suggests that 97 percent of those surveyed support sex education in the schools. One respondent wrote, "I had sex education in my junior year of high school and by then it was a joke. Most of the people in the class were involved in sexual relationships and one person already had a baby."

But how is sex education to be handled? Jacqueline Kasun, a Humboldt (Calif.) State University economics professor, believes sex education courses turn children into sex experts. She argues that sex education "has become a 'movement,' the focus of which is less biological than political. Its prime movers are mainly psychologists, sociologists and 'health

educators' concerned less with the psychology of pro-
creation than with 'value clarification.'"[10] But a Seattle
boy told *Newsweek*, "They taught me about all the
body parts . . . but what is sex?" Sociologist Frank F.
Furstenberg, Jr., of the University of Pennsylvania,
says, "It's safe to teach the mechanics of reproduction
but threatening to talk about values and responsibilities."[11]

I have personally interviewed a number of Wheaton
College students who took sex education courses in
high school, and not one felt that the course addressed
anything more than the mechanics of sex. Nevertheless, this does not mean that secularists have no plans
to introduce the question of value into sex education.
Kasun states, "In undertaking to finance and promote
a multi-million-dollar program of sex education, the
government has entered very heavily into the promotion of a particular world-view and the establishment of
a chosen ideology, a kind of secular religion."[12]

Indeed, one California-based textbook, which has
since been banned, suggested that "if an adolescent
really feels O.K. about having sex, then advance planning should not be a major problem." The same book
told students that it should consider a wide variety of
lifestyles, including homosexuality, communes, group
marriages and couples living together without marriage.[13]

It is this kind of approach to sex education that
caused Robert Grant, the president of American Christian Cause, to call for a "National Decency in Education
Sunday." He said, "America's children are in grave
danger, and their parents are often not even aware of
what they are being taught in the classroom."[14]

What does an authentic Christian humanism have
to say about sex education? Certainly Christians are
not opposed to children's learning about sex in a struc-
tured setting. *Newsweek* reports that good programs

in sex education begin long before puberty. For example, in Palatine, Illinois, plant reproduction is learned by first graders. By the time they are in sixth grade, they study animal and human reproduction, anatomy, puberty, and body changes. Other high schools have opened on-site clinics for instruction and birth control. Statistics show that the pregnancy rates in these schools declined 40 percent in three years.

Some schools are even taking the step of including children and parents in the same course. In St. Paul, Minnesota, for example, a Roman Catholic school puts the parents through the sex education courses before their ninth graders take it. Part of the assignment is to discuss the lessons at home.

Traditionally, Christian churches and families have shied away from sex education. Perhaps it is time to develop a curriculum for church and home where sexual values can be taught in an open and supportive atmosphere—a place where people can be comfortable talking about sex. Surely this domain of life also belongs to the Creator, and we have a responsibility— nay, a duty—to instruct and clarify sexual issues in church and home.

SCIENTIFIC CREATIONISM

A third arena of conflict between Christians and secularists is the issue of evolution versus scientific creationism. This issue was first brought to national attention in the so-called Scopes II Trial in California in 1981.

Kelly Segraves, a member of the Creation Science Research Center, accused the State of California of violating the religious freedom of his children by teaching evolution as a fact. Segraves settled for the recommendation that teachers should quality their assertions about science by saying "most scientists believe" or "scientists hypothesize."[15]

The issue is not really "creation versus evolution." Rather, it is that evolution should not be taught as factual science. Christians who advocate this point of view were supported by Ronald Reagan in his presidential election campaign: "I have a great many questions about it [evolution]. I think that recent discoveries down through the years have pointed up great flaws in it."[16]

Creationists are not casting the battle, like the original Scopes Trial, in terms of "who's right." Their tactic is to argue that the "two-model theory" of creation be taught. That is, alongside of evolution, which must be viewed as a theory, should be taught another theory, which argues from a scientific point of view for the sudden and fairly recent creation of the world. Consequently the push by creationists is for "equal time." The dictum of constitutional neutrality, they say, requires that the government not take sides on a religious question.

Henry Morris of the University of Minnesota, a former evolutionist, states that his study of the Bible and science caused him to see that evolution is a religion—for humanists and atheists.

A strict nontheistic evolution is indeed religious. If, as nontheistic evolutionists affirm, the world is the result of chance or some impersonal force, a view of the world results that can properly be called religious (even though it has no established organization and rituals). A belief in nontheistic evolution demands particular conclusions regarding the origin of the world, the nature of man, the process of history, the rise of religious institutions, and the end of the world. These viewpoints determine one's world-view and in turn affect attitudes toward personal morality and public policy.

But the ACLU has challenged the notion of the religious nature of evolution in the courts of Arkansas where a new law was passed in 1981 that requires "balanced treatment of creation-science and evolution-science in public schools" (Act 590).

The ACLU contended that scientific creationism "establishes religion in the schools and thus violates the First and Fourteenth Amendments of the Constitution." The ACLU complaint charged that the act was "Conceived and drafted by employees of 'creationism' organizations who subscribe to a 'fundamentalist' religious belief that the universe, energy and life were all created suddenly by a Divine Creator, as described in Genesis. These same 'creationism' organizations produce and sell for profit 'Creationism' textbooks and materials, and would therefore profit financially from the passage and implementation of the Creationism Act."[17]

In January 1982 a federal judge declared Act 590 unconstitutional on the grounds that creationism is religious in nature and constitutes bad science.

The issue for Christians is a difficult one, because not all Christians believe in scientific creationism and don't wish to be pushed into that mold. The attitude that scientific creationism is the only alternative to a godless evolutionary theory, with all its implications for secularism, is not acceptable to numerous Christians. Many agree with the statement of Pope John Paul II that "the Bible itself speaks to us of the origin of the universe and its makeup, not in order to provide us with a scientific treatise, but in order to state the correct relationship of man with God and with the universe."[18]

Many evangelical scientists, theologians, and laypeople agree with the intent of the Pope's statement. It asserts that the essential nature of the biblical story of Creation is religious and not scientific. Its concern is to emphasize the *who* of Creation and not the *when* or the *how*. For this reason many conservative Christians do not want to be associated with the rigid attitude of scientific creationism toward a young earth or a seven-literal-days theory of Creation. Consequently there are evangelical scientists who affirm the long-day theory of Creation (each day representing a long or indefinite period of time) and there are some who believe that evolution and creation are not contradictory, affirming a theistic evolution.

The real issue for Christians, then, is not a matter of teaching a two-model theory, but a teaching of science that allows for the element of theory in the evolutionary hypothesis. How this will be treated in the classroom will more than likely depend on the commitment of the teacher. Perhaps the Christian community should be more concerned to challenge young people to consider the teaching of science in public schools as a Christian vocation.

PRAYER AND RELIGIOUS OBSERVANCE

Prayer in the public schools was an established custom in this country until only recently. Colonial statutes providing for daily prayer in the classroom date as far back as 1684. But in the 1960s, the U.S. Supreme Court issued rulings on prayer and Bible reading that led to legislation forbidding these religious exercises in public schools. Many Christians saw this as further evidence of the takeover in education by secular humanists.

There are two major philosophies about religion in public education. One says that government engages in public education because it is the best way to provide education for all the people. The second says that education is an intrinsic activity of the state designed to create a uniform mentality among the citizens. In America, the former rather than the latter position has been the predominant view. Now the question is, *Should government protect freedom* from *religion or freedom* of *religion in the public schools?*

The abandonment of required prayer, the agitation against religious symbols during religious holidays, and the freedom to have religious meetings on a public campus raise this issue. Recent legislation seems to suggest that the government should protect the freedom *of* religion rather than freedom from religion. First, the Helms Amendment now pending would, if ratified, forbid the Supreme Court to hear any case involving prayer in a public school or a public building. U.S. Senator Jesse Helms, sponsor of the amendment, wants schools to be free to allow each class to have one minute each day for voluntary prayer. Christian humanists see little point in this exercise. They agree with columnist James J. Kilpatrick, a Roman Catholic, that "the prayers contemplated by the Senator are bound by their very nature to be little more than ritual prayers, perfunctory prayers—the kind of prayers denounced in Matthew 6:5-6."[19] Children are already allowed to pray. What the Helms Amendment would do is to require prayers written and sponsored by government. Christians should oppose this kind of token religious exercise as more damaging than profitable.

But there is another issue of recent importance in which Christians did not and should not stand quietly by. I speak of the liberty of Christians to meet for prayer and Bible study in public schools. A case in point is the refusal of the Kansas City campus of the University of Missouri to allow a group of Christian students to meet for prayer and study in a public classroom. The case went all the way to the U.S. Supreme Court, which in late 1981 ruled in favor of the Christians. Associate Justice Lewis Powell stated in the decision, "The question is not whether the creation of a religious forum would violate the Establishment Clause [of the U.S. Constitution].[20] He wrote, "The university has opened its facilities for use by student groups, and the question is whether it can now exclude groups because of the content of their speech."[21] This ruling allows schools to observe religious holidays for both Christians and Jews and permits religious groups free expression in public places.

CONCLUSION

We have seen that the conflict between secular humanists and Christian humanists is building in public education. This is a summary of the matters about which we need to be concerned:

- The teaching of values without reference to an objective standard of right and wrong.

- The teaching of sex without respect for morality and without understanding the need for the maturing mind to learn how to make decisions based on moral restraint.

- The teaching of origin and meaning of man's existence from an evolutionary standpoint without reference to a possible transcendent Creator and meaning-giver.

- The task of government is to protect the freedom of religion, not freedom from religion. A case in point is prayer and the observance of religious traditions during holy seasons.

It is very difficult to determine the extent to which secularism has permeated the educational institutions of this country. Informal contacts with principals of schools in the Chicago area seem to suggest that the issue is not quite so critical as the religious right makes it out to be. Said one principal, "Most of the teachers in this country are so busy worrying about lesson plans, maintaining order in the classroom, and parent conferences, that they don't have time to think through the theoretical questions."

It may very well be that the advocates of secularism are in an ivory tower writing books and agenda for teachers who have little time or concern for a secularist agenda. Yet there are those who are committed to challenging a Christian value system or who, by their lack of personal commitment to Judeo-Christian values, undermine them inadvertently. Whatever the case, it is well for Christians and the church to be informed of the potential threat of secularism in public education.

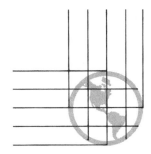

7

The Political Tangle

The emergence of fundamentalism as a political force in America came as a great surprise to many in the late seventies. "The moralists in America have had enough," said Jerry Falwell. "We are joining hands together for the changing, the rejuvenating of a nation."[1] So Falwell and other fundamentalist leaders stormed the halls of Congress with what they called a "divine mandate" to clean up America.

This eruption of fundamentalist political activity caused a huge stir among its opponents. One major cry against the religious right has been against its so-called mixture of politics and religion. To this Jerry Falwell retorted, "Nobody's ever accused the National Council of Churches of mixing religion and politics. . . . But when ol' Jerry gets into it, that's violating separation of church and state. The problem isn't violating anything. The problem is that we don't agree with those buzzards—and that we outnumber them."[2]

Evangelist James Robison agrees. "It's time for God's people to come out of the closet and the churches—and change America," he thundered to 15,000 people in Dallas in the summer of 1980.

But Bartlett Giamatti, president of Yale University, views the situation differently. "What disgusts me so much about the 'morality' seeping out of the ground around our feet is that it would deny the legitimacy of differences," he wrote to the incoming freshmen in 1981. "Whatever view does not conform to these [new right] views is by definition relativistic, negative, secular, immoral, against the family, anti-free enterprise, un-American. What nonsense. What dangerous malicious nonsense," he concluded.[3]

Here we see the clash of systems in the political arena. So we must ask, How involved should the church and Christians be in using political means to establish morality in the social order? And basic to this question is another: What is the relationship of the church to the state?

Figure 7

LEGISLATING MORALITY

The point at which the Christian and secularist views of governing are clashing most severely is the issue over the use of political power to legislate morality. The clash is most vividly seen in laws regarding homosexuality, abortion, marriage, and euthanasia. The Christian believes the Bible and Christian custom have set forth some "absolutes" in these matters. The secularist believes that moral law should reflect the practice and conviction of the general public. For secularists, laws are relative and determined ultimately by the people, not by God.

Thus secularists who are committed to a view that people ought to be free to do whatever they want to do are coming into increasing conflict with Christians who believe in moral absolutes and want the government to restrain sin for the common good.

Francis Canavan, S.J., professor of political science at Fordham University, attacks the freedom argument of secularists in an article called "The Dilemma of Liberal Pluralism."[4] The government, he argues, simply cannot be neutral. If its task is to promote the welfare of the people, then it must have an opinion regarding the substance of that welfare.

For example, *the debate over homosexuality* is not a neutral issue, nor is it a matter dealing only with the freedom of gay people to express their sexual commitment openly without harrassment from the government or society. The assertion that homosexuality and heterosexuality are of equal value will have far-reaching social consequences. For the government to pass laws making them of equal value puts the government in a position of supporting a particular lifestyle and relativizing heterosexual relationships. Thus Christians and secularists disagree on laws regarding homosexuality. One side wants to protect the normative value of heterosexual relations; the other wants to affirm the ultimacy of freedom for the individual.

A second example may be drawn from *the abortion issue.* When the U.S. Supreme Court decided in 1973 that abortion is a constitutional right, there followed a huge battle over the public funding of abortions. In this case the state did not take a "neutral" position regarding human life. By affirming the "rights" of the woman over her body, the government devalued prenatal human life. The unborn child has no right in and of itself; its right is only determined by the value that the mother gives to it. Consequently, under the law, abortion became a positive good that the state is called upon to subsidize for the good of its citizens.

A third example can be drawn from *the institution of marriage.* In this country the law has been based upon marriage as a legal contract containing rights and obligations not given to other human relationships. However, this arrangement is now being challenged by court decisions that support the rights of those who co-habit without the legal sanction of marriage. An example of this is found in the suit filed against actor Lee Marvin by his lover of six years. His lover had first to establish her right to sue. The California Supreme Court, in awarding her the right to sue, noted that the law should not "impose a standard based on alleged moral considerations that have apparently been so widely abandoned by so many."[5]

In writing this law, the Supreme Court of California institutionalized and affirmed an extramarital relationship, making it "the basis of legal rights, and thereby changed the status of marriage in American law."[6] One law, which had longstanding tradition in American history, was substituted for a new law under the assumption that the changing pattern of people's lives determines what is right and wrong. The courts, having no objective standard, allow the social mores of the day to determine moral law.

The same is true of *euthanasia*. Joseph Sobran, a syndicated columnist and contributing editor to the *Human Life Review*, says, "To institutionalize suicide means not only to permit it, but also to *encourage* it."[7] The point is that in a secular society, once something is made legal, it becomes ethical.

These illustrations point to the deeper issue going on in the current conflict between Christian and secular views of the state and its role in changing the laws that affect the morals of this country. Unfortunately, the arguments of the conservatives frequently sound as though they want to coerce or manipulate others to their point of view. Consequently the bellicose language gets in the way of real communication.

What we must face, at the bottom line, is that Christians and secularists are looking at the same issues through different pairs of glasses. The Christian sees the role of government under God to maintain laws that reflect the Judeo-Christian heritage of the

West. But the secularist, not accepting a notion of transcendence, advocates an individualistic notion of freedom and calls upon the government to protect the right of every individual to assert and to live by his or her own values.

SEPARATION OF CHURCH AND STATE

"There are some problems . . . which can only be solved by indirect deductions from what the New Testament says. There are other problems which are actually posed and solved by the New Testament. *The question of church and state is one of them,*" writes Oscar Cullmann, a renowned New Testament scholar.[8]

What does the New Testament teach about the state?

The State Is a Temporary Institution

An authentic Christian humanism recognizes that the ultimate rule is the kingdom of God. For this reason, Christians view the state as an order that belongs to the present age, an authority that will vanish when the kingdom comes. Consequently Christians are placed in a position to actually judge the state. Jesus said, "Give to Caesar what is Caesar's, and to God what is God's" (Luke 20:25). In this statement Jesus recognized the state as a temporary institution and was unwilling to join the zealots who wanted to overthrow the Roman government to establish the kingdom of God. Furthermore, he acknowledged that we ought to give the state what it needs for its existence. For this reason Christians are to pay their taxes and pray for the state (1 Tim. 2:1-2).

But Jesus did not, either by words or by actions, advocate a state nationalism on the part of Christians. The attempt to establish the kingdom of God through any or all efforts of Christians to control the state is a denial of the temporal nature of the state. It is a sellout to "civil religion" that fails to maintain the true "other-worldly" character of Christianity, which sees ultimate power as belonging to God and his kingdom that is yet to come.

John R. W. Stott, rector emeritus of All Souls Church, London, has criticized the nationalistic fervor of the religious right. "What we are seeing," he said, "both in your country and mine, is a resurgence of nationalism rather than a resurgence of Christianity." He defines nationalism as "my country right or wrong" and patriotism as "an uncritical love of country." He warned that "if you love Christ and love your country, you should not be so involved as an American citizen that you cannot stand back and look at it objectively." He declared that, for a Christian, "the Lordship of Jesus should permeate the whole of life and make him critical of every other loyalty."[9] The point is that our ultimate loyalty is to Christ and his kingdom and not to America—which, like other nation-states, will not endure forever. Therefore, the Christian who knows that America is temporary does not give it his ultimate allegiance and remains critical toward it in light of his allegiance to the kingdom.

The State Is Part of the Fallen Order and Can Therefore Be Used As an Effective Tool of Satan

In the three Pauline statements that speak of the state (Rom. 13:1ff.; 1 Cor. 2:8; 6:1ff.), there is an allusion to the angelic powers that stand behind the state. For English readers today, the term "rulers of the world" means little more than "the political rulers of our time." However, for Jewish readers, this phrase meant what Paul talks about in Ephesians 6:12: The rulers are the "demonic, invisible powers which stand behind all earthly happenings and use human beings as their effective agents."[10]

Certainly this is the way the apostle John sees the

Roman state in the Apocalypse. There the state demands what belongs to God and becomes a satanic power. So Cullmann writes, "It is characteristic that government power exceeding its proper bounds is generally regarded as the most tangible embodiment of satanic power."[11] For John, the powerful engagement of the state in its attempt to destroy the church is the expression of institutionalized evil. This most clearly expresses itself in the emergence of a totalitarian state.

Totalitarianism is an attempt to imitate God. The state has all the answers. It rules over every aspect of life and controls all aspects of the social order under the pretense of the "common good." This totalitarian state even takes on a religious character (see Rev. 16:13; 19:20; 20:10). The false prophet stands in the place of God and declares himself to be God. The ethical distinction between good and evil falls away, and whatever the state declares to be right becomes right. Surely this is the direction in which secularism, having no objective power over the state, is leading the world. The state, as we see in the writings of Machiavelli, becomes an end in itself. Whatever it decides is right is right. Christians must be alert to this possibility and aware that the elevation of the state to a position of ultimate power is satanic.

The Existence and Responsibility of the State Within the Social Order Is Willed by God

In Romans 13:1-7, Paul admonishes the Christians of his day to affirm that the state is willed or ordained by God (see also 1 Peter 2:13-17). But the purpose of the state, according to Paul, is quite limited. It is to administer justice. What does this mean? According to the Association for Public Justice, a Christian political organization, "The proper task of the state is to bind together, in a public legal community, all persons, groups and institutions within its territory." This means a rejection of both "individualistic" and "collectivistic" political ideologies.

For example, individualism, following the teaching of John Locke, views the state as an artificial creation of individuals. People define the state's purpose, limits, and powers. This is an Enlightenment view which argues, as we do in America, that government is "of the people, by the people, and for the people." This is a secular view of government that gives ultimate power to the people. If the desires and convictions of the people change, the government and its laws may change to reflect the convictions of the people for whom the government exists.

On the other hand, a collectivist ideology—like communism—which is opposed to individualism, elevates the "society" to a position of ultimate power. Communists destroy diversity in an attempt to attain uniformity and equality of all people. The government or "elite" ruling power determines what is good for the whole and attempts to impose that "good" on all through its laws. This is another kind of secularism, because it does not recognize the sovereignty of God over the state and all else.

An authentic Christian humanism acknowledges the great diversity of the social order and argues that the state is not to control this diversity. Rather, the state is to govern in such a way as to protect the interests of each group. So the state, which is the political community, consists of family, church, educational institutions, unions, and various other volunteer associations. The government, which is the office of authority in the state, must hold these groups together in the tension that exists between freedom and order.

That being the case, what is the responsibility of government from a Christian point of view? It should be seen as an authority appointed by God. Because man is made in the image of God and is given freedom, government should not seek to control other human beings as though it has some "right" over them. For this reason, Christians view the office of governmental authority as one of service. The purpose of government is not to control or manipulate the people, but to serve their needs, to make certain that each group has an opportunity to be heard and to have its "rights" protected within the law. Consequently government ought not to be the rule of a "majority" as much as it ought to be a rule for all people seeking to serve their genuine needs and concerns.

CONCLUSION

The battle between the secularists and Christian humanists is bound to take place in part in the political arena. Here are the main ideas to keep in mind:

- When a homosexual lifestyle, abortion, cohabitation without marriage, euthanasia, and other such moral issues are made legal by the courts, they will ultimately be regarded as ethical.

- The responsibility of the state in a pluralistic society is to protect the interests of all legitimate associations and groupings of people in such a way that both freedom and order are maintained.

The concern of moral legislation and the relationship between church and state is not easy to resolve. Throughout history a number of models between church and government have existed. What has always been constant in these varying situations is the obligation of the Christians to pray for those who rule over them and to exercise their right of citizenship for the welfare of all the people.

III

The Church in a Secular Society

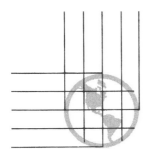

8

Where Do We Go From Here?

Before we answer the question "Where do we go from here?" it will be helpful to summarize the key themes developed in this book.

- We live in a post-Christian era. The notion of a Christian society is an ideal of the past in the West.

- The process of secularization has driven a wedge between the "secular " and the "sacred."

- The dominant impulse that gives shape to our secular society is a nontheistic humanism.

- Secular humanism, one of many different forms of humanism, represents a minority viewpoint among humanists. But its proponents are vocal, strident, and characterized by evangelistic fervor.

- Recently the religious right has singled out secular humanism as its special target. The secularists have responded in kind.

- The "clash of systems" is occurring in the moral sphere, in the social order, in the educational system, and in the political order.

Two world-view systems like Christian humanism and secular humanism existing in the same society will continue to clash. Christian humanism and secular humanism are not only dramatically opposed systems, they also produce opposite ways of unfolding culture. Consequently the development of society cannot be "neutral." If persons are bent toward evil, then the society they create will express that evil. On the other hand, if persons are committed to goodness, the impact they make on the unfolding process of society will reflect that goodness.

FOUR REASONS WHY THE SYSTEMS WILL CONTINUE TO CLASH

If it is inevitable that the systems will continue to clash, there must be some reasons inherent within each system that will provoke the conflict. There are four.

Human Nature Is Fallen

Christian humanists believe human nature is fallen, but secular humanists believe in the inherent goodness of man. Scripture everywhere teaches that the Fall is so pervasive that it extends not only to humans, but also to their cultural unfolding, to the society and culture which they create (Rom. 1:18-3:23; Eph. 2:1-3). In this sense, society may be regarded as an "extension of man." The lust, greed, hate, violence, selfishness, inhumanity, and dishonesty of the individual finds expression in the institutional organizations of human beings. Therefore the state goes to war, families are destroyed by divorce, innocent people are cheated, and poor people are oppressed. Scripture is also clear that this kind of society will continue until the end of history. All naïve hopes that individuals will change and society will become better are utopian and false.

Christ Has Redeemed the World

Christian humanists believe Christ is the Redeemer of the world, but secular humanists believe the salvation of the world is a human task. The Scriptures do not set God and the world (the created order) against each other. Rather, Scripture unites God and the world in the Incarnation, where God actually assumed flesh in the man, Christ Jesus. Christ's incarnation, death, and resurrection are "world affirming," not "world rejecting." Christ is the salvation of the world, the one who restores it and renews it, and the one who will someday completely release it from its bondage to sin (Rom. 8:18-25).

The Church Is the Society of the Redeemed

Christian humanists believe the church is the society of the redeemed, but secular humanists regard the church as the enemy of progress. Scripture affirms the unique nature of the church in more than eighty different images. Most agree that the most important image is that of the "body" (Eph. 5). The implication of this image is that the church is the extension of Jesus in the world. As Jesus loved and affirmed mankind and the world, so the church loves and serves the world. It cares about the needs of the poor, the hungry, the outcast and the oppressed. In this sense the church is the mirror *What Ought to Be* in the midst of *What Is.*

The Church Is to Act As "Salt" and "Light"

Christian humanists believe the church is called to act as "salt" and "light," to witness to its hope, and to restrain evil, but secular humanists believe the church stands in the way of freedom. If the church is to *be* Christ to the world, it has a task. Ministering to the world and caring for the world in the name of Christ implies an active engagement in every area of human life and vocation. The ideal is for the Christian to permeate all of life, sharing in its failures, experiences, and successes—always bringing into it the continued presence of its loving and recreating Lord.

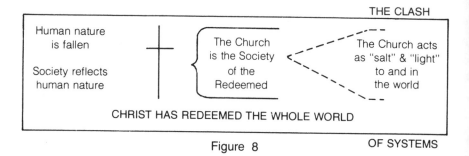

Figure 8

WHAT THE CHURCH SHOULD NOT DO IN SOCIETY

It is an old saying that anything which is good in and of itself can be subject to misuse and therefore become evil (i.e., 1 Cor. 6:12-14). Unfortunately this is true of Christian humanism as much as anything else. When the church compromises its essential message and purpose in the world, or when it seeks to fulfill its mission to the world through some worldly means, the church will adopt a stance either of accommodation or of mere confrontation with the world.

William Druel of Chicago put his finger on the problem rather succinctly when he wrote that the Christian church finds itself "somewhere between a posture that accommodates the system and a stance which totally condemns it."[1]

Homer Duncan, director of Missionary Crusader, accuses the liberal church of an accommodation to the system. He claims that "they turned aside to a social gospel and allowed the enemies of Christ to infiltrate Christian seminaries, then the churches. If the ministers in our churches had stood firmly on the Word of God, the enemies that are now destroying our society would have been driven back."[2]

On the other hand, Spurgeon Dunnam III, editor of the *National Christian Reporter,* responding negatively to the harsh criticisms of Jerry Falwell against our society, issued Falwell a challenge to debate. Dunnam said that the challenge stemmed from a "conviction that the 'Moral Majority' has come to epitomize a type of political activity draped in religious terminology which I consider fundamentally at odds in many respects with the gospel of our Lord Jesus Christ."[3]

Both Duncan and Dunnam have a point. Their observations lead to two assertions about the relationship of Christianity to society that must be kept in mind as we consider the future response of the church to the world.

- The church should not enter into political and economic alliances that will compromise authentic Christian humanism.
- The church should not seek to accomplish its task in society through political power or legislative force.

An Example From History

Mark Noll, professor of history at Wheaton College, provides us with an excellent example from American history regarding the use of political power. In a paper entitled, "Christianity and Humanistic Values in Eighteenth-Century America,"[4] he gives an analysis that is of double value to us, because this is the century during which the United States came into existence. His observations help to deal with the question of whether or not the United States was founded as a Christian nation.

Christian humanism of the eighteenth-century was the direct heir of Puritanism, which "showed its humanistic bent through its comprehensive outlook on man, his world, and the human condition in that world."[5] Building on this vision, the church expressed a resolve to purify society at large and Christianize America as much as possible.

At the beginning of the eighteenth-century, however, "autonomous humanism seemed to be replacing the Christian humanism of the Puritan Way."[6] The rise of satire against the church by people like Benjamin Franklin and the general spread of deistic ideas brought the influence of Puritan Christian humanism nearly to an end.

It was in this context that the Great Awakening of the 1730s and 1740s came. The leaders of the revival movement turned away from the "comprehensive vision of human society" taught in Christian humanism and sought instead to promote "personal religion."[7] In doing so, personal, private religion increased while secularism continued on the rise. By the mid-fifties a situation existed not unsimilar to that in America today: Religion and secularism were both increasing in parallel movements. (This, of course, is bound to happen when religion is not related to the social order.)

Because the concern for a Christian impact on society was not completely dead, Christians who were committed to an authentic humanism became convinced that the best way they could accomplish their goals in society was to enter into an alliance with the Whig Party. They were attracted to the Whigs, because "they looked at political power through humanistic spectacles. Rightly used, political power would ensure human liberty; it would encourage human virtue; it would preserve human rights."[8]

Unfortunately the Whigs who were humanists were not Christians. Eventually a situation was created in which the Whig philosophy of life came into competition with Christian humanism, overcoming it and perverting it.

There are a number of specific ways in which eighteenth-century Christianity became perverted through its alliance with politics. For example, the nationalism of Christians who were in support of Whig ideology prevented them from seeing the possible flaws in the concept of revolution. Gradually, therefore, the humanism of Whiggery became "lord" over Christian humanism. Consequently Christian humanism became "unbalanced," and many Christians eventually abandoned their faith in favor of "the precepts of Whig ideology as the final arbiter of behavior." The result was not the Christian renaissance for which many hoped. Rather, the non-Christian ideas of the Enlightenment gained a more firm foothold in American soil, introducing "the low water marks in American history for church membership."[9]

This conformity to Whig humanism affected the Christian faith in at least five ways. First, it led to a corrupt use of the Bible in which the Beast of Revelation was identified with the British people. Second, it resulted in the debasement of theology to the point where the Presbyterian synod of New York and Philadelphia threatened to break off ecclesiastical fellowship with the synod of North Carolina, if it did not support the patriotic cause. Third, it adversely affected ecclesiastical unity and fellowship. Fourth, it led to "the establishment of Whig values as the ultimate standards of approval before God." And finally, it perverted authentic Christian humanism.[10]

This brief excursion into eighteenth-century American history should alert Christians to the possible way in which the religious right today may be making similar mistakes. It would be foolish indeed not to take the warnings of history seriously.

A Contemporary Example

If well-intentioned Christians of the eighteenth century made the mistake of entering into an alliance that eventually did damage to the Christian cause, there is little reason to believe that the same thing could not occur today. Frankly, a similar alliance seems to have been developing between conservative political and religious movements in recent years.

The underlying issue of this alliance is the asser-
tion that America has a religious destiny. In *Listen*
America, Jerry Falwell writes, "Our founding Fathers
firmly believed that America had a special destiny in the
world."[11] He also writes, "I am positive in my belief regarding the constitution that God led in the development of that document."[12] This is a view set forth by the
leaders of the new Christian right with near-absolute
consistency. There is a commitment to Americanism
that goes far beyond what a true Christian humanism
would allow. James Dunn, the executive director of the
Christian Life Commission of the Baptist General Convention of Texas, put it this way: "We wind up making
God the national mascot, and that's civil religion at its
worst."[13] There are several dangerous implications to
this revival of religious nationalism that need to be considered seriously by the Christian who cares for an authentic Christian humanism.

First, religious nationalism attributes to the na-
tion what the New Testament ascribes to the church.
It is not God's intention to save the world through
America. His salvation, which is rooted in Jesus
Christ, is proclaimed by the church. Paul is explicit in
Ephesians that the "power" which belongs to Jesus by
virtue of his death and resurrection is given to the
church "which is his body, the fullness of him who fills
everything in every way" (1:23). He goes on to say that
"his intent was that now, through the church, the
manifold wisdom of God should be made known to the
rulers and authorities in the heavenly realms" (3:10).

Yet a group known as Christian Heritage in San
Jose, California, is circulating a pamphlet entitled
"The U.S. in Bible Prophecy," in which they insist that
we Americans are the "ten lost tribes of Israel" and that
"we are under the responsibility to live up to the conditions imposed upon us by our position in the world as

the dominant or 'chosen' race as set out in the Bible."[14]

Religious nationalism is also promoted by Jerry Falwell. In an interview in *Christianity Today,* Falwell said that "God has raised up America for the cause of world evangelization and for the protection of his people, the Jews. I don't think America has any other right or reason for existence other than these two purposes."[15] Christian humanists' response to this is that the task of the world evangelization was given to the church, not to America, and the protection of the Jews is ultimately in God's hand of Providence, not in the military might of America. If these ideas are taken seriously by the religious right, then they have perverted the gospel of Jesus Christ and turned it into "another gospel" (Gal. 1:6).

Second, *religious nationalism has the effect of wedding the church to the political right.* It is a matter of interest that the American government almost always seeks some kind of religious sanction. Unfortunately for the church, its fortunes seem to rise or fall with those of the particular party it blesses. This was the case with the alliance between theological liberals and the New Deal inaugurated by President Franklin Delano Roosevelt. When Roosevelt's brand of "socialism" fell in the 1970s, the Christian establishment fell with it.

Interestingly the rise of the political right and Ronald Reagan has produced another religious phenomenon to bless and sanction the new policies of government. This time the "baptism" comes from the religious right. "You can't be a good Christian and a liberal at the same time," says Jerry Falwell.[16]

Evangelist Billy Graham, whose public standing was affected as a result of his relationship with President Richard Nixon, is more cautious. In *Parade* magazine, a supplement to many Sunday newspapers, Graham said of a conversation he had with Falwell, "I told him to preach the Gospel. That's our calling. I want to preserve the purity of the Gospel and the freedom of religion in America . . . , but it would disturb me if there was a wedding between the religious fundamentalists and the political right. The hard right has no interest in religion except to manipulate it."[17]

The alliance with the political right developing today may be similar to that of the Christians with the Whigs in the eighteenth century. I find it difficult to develop confidence in the political right's "Christian" intention when one of its leaders, Richard Vigarie, states, "We've already taken control of the conservative movement. And conservatives have taken control of the Republican Party. The remaining thing is to see if we can take control of this country."[18]

If the religious right succeeds in doing this, let us hope that the rhetoric of Paul Weyrich, director of the Committee for the Survival of a Free Congress, does not come true. He says, "We're radicals working to overturn the present structure in this country . . . we're talking about Christianizing America."[19] This may sound like a good goal, but its results will not be healthy for the church and an authentic Christian humanism, much less the freedom of those who disagree.

Third, religious nationalism that baptizes Americanism will eventually politicize the church. I'm not the kind of person who writes letters to magazines, either when I agree or when I disagree with their editorials or articles. However, in the case of the September 8, 1981, interview with Jerry Falwell, which appeared in *Christianity Today,* I did write. Frankly, I was appalled by the magazine's failure to provide a critical assessment of Falwell's view of America and his totally neglecting to mention the church. Here is part of my letter, which speaks for itself.

> I want to be critical of Falwell's argument that God's role for America is to bring spiritual renewal to the world. He

confuses America with the church. The point is that despite Falwell's insistence that the Moral Majority "Americanism" is separate from the church, it is in fact a movement largely among the fundamentalist churches and represents a fundamentalist political ideology.

Consequently, it alters the fundamental nature and mission of the church away from evangelism, education, worship and fellowship. Instead Falwellian Fundamentalism tends to turn local churches into political power bases, special agents of capitalist economics, champions of liberty, moral legislators, defenders of messianic Americanism and advocates of militarism.

This letter may sound as though I am fighting the Moral Majority. Quite frankly, I am supportive of the Moral Majority in many of its issues. What is being fought for here is the *church* —and ultimately the freedom of the church to act in a prophetic manner consistent with an authentic Christian humanism.

Fourth, religious nationalism will lead the church into uncritical support of militaristic policies. The theology of the religious right requires that it support a strong America and the buildup of its defenses around the world. For example, Falwell argues that the great revival which will come to this world "somewhere between here and the Rapture" will occur through America. "God's role for America," he says, "is as catalyst, that he wants to set the spiritual time bomb off right here." He continues, "If that is the case, then America must stay free."[20]

Any good American does not want to see America destroyed. However, Christian support of military might, questionable as that may be, becomes even more suspect when it is set forth on the pious premise that "God wants to set the spiritual time bomb off right here."

Again, what is at stake is the view of the church. If

America were to fall tomorrow, God's work in the world would continue. He has not appointed this country to save the world, nor to be the chief exponent of his saving grace to the world. This is the task of the church which knows no national or cultural boundaries. To protect "God's interests" with "military might" is therefore a blasphemy against his church, which is the instrument of God's proclamation to the world.

WHAT THE CHURCH CAN AND SHOULD DO IN SOCIETY

The New Testament draws a distinction between the church in its institutional function and the church in its function as the people of God. In its institutional function, the church is to evangelize, worship, teach, and administer its inner life. Thus, as an institution the church should seek no earthly political power, because it belongs to the kingdom which is not of this world (John 17:14) and has no affinity with the powers which rule this world (Eph. 2:2).

On the other hand, the church also functions in the world as the people of God. In this way the church enters every sphere of life through its people who live and work in the political arena, in the social and economic order, in the field of education, and within the conflict of moral choices that must be made at work or in the family. Therefore the church as people are in constant confrontation with the fallen powers which control every level of the social order (Eph. 6:12).

Now, we must ask the question, "What can the church do in society?" This question will be answered on both the institutional and personal levels.

What the Church As an Institution Can Do

It has already been made clear that the institutional church should not align itself with a particular political party as a means of making its impact on society. The Reverend Jimmy Allen of Fort Worth, Texas, registered his complaint against the new religious right and partisan politics this way: What is supposed to be "a non-partisan movement for Jesus . . . always seems to turn into a Republican rally."[21]

If the institutional church ought not to choose sides politically as a way of accomplishing its goals, what should it do?

First, the church ought to take a more aggressive role in teaching Christian values. One of the great conflicts between the church and society in general lies in the matter of values. The church ought to tap into its rich treasury of values, which it has received from the Old Testament law and the example of Jesus, and prepare an agenda for the teaching of "Christian values clarification." In this way the people of God can become more fully sensitized to the clash of values between Christianity and secularism and find support through the local church for the stands that Christians take in society.

It is imperative, however, that the church not make the error of teaching legalism. Legalism and the Christian value system are two different things. Legalism is a handy list of do's and don'ts; it says do not smoke or drink, go to dances, or play cards. Although Christians should not disregard the dangers inherent in these practices, many groups so emphasize these matters and make them a primary means of judging faith that they miss the weightier matters. People who obey all the secondary rules may feel smug and spiritual because they are fulfilling all the proscribed duties. Yet they may harbor feelings of racism, prejudice against women, indifference to the suffering of the poor and needy, and live for fast cars, sporty clothes, and expensive vacations. In other words, there is a kind of "Christian playboy mentality" that frequently goes unchallenged as long as the "right"

legalistic features of the "in" spirituality are obviously
adhered to.

An authentic Christian humanism will express a
biblical and historic spirituality over against the immature and irresponsible spirituality of legalistic Christianity. Its deepest concern is to call people into the
fullness of a life instructed by the Holy Spirit. The ultimate values of the church are those that are exem-
plified in Jesus Christ and communicated by the Holy
Spirit. Simple as it may sound, Christians must learn
to live by the fruit of the Holy Spirit. The ultimate in
Christian values is "love, joy, peace, patience, kindness, goodness, faithfulness, gentleness and self-
control" (Gal. 5:22). If we want the secular world to
respect the Christian faith and to be drawn to it, we
must begin again with the basics. We must learn how
to *live* in imitation of Christ, by the power of the Holy
Spirit.

*Second, the institutional church can and should
act as a social critic.* The church has the responsibility
not only to make its positive values clear, but also to
identify sin in all its forms—personal and social. Vermont Royster, columnist for *The Wall Street Journal,*
puts it this way: "If the Catholic Church believes that
abortion is morally evil, then it has the right—nay, the
duty—of its cardinals to say so and to urge their flock
to oppose those who would make it acceptable public
policy."[22]

If the church as an institution should act as a social critic, the question is how? Figure 9 indicates five
ways.

Pat Robertson, host of "The 700 Club," said there
is a better way than "active partisan politics." It is, he
said, "Fasting and praying . . . appealing, in essence,
to a higher power." Next, the church ought to recover
the social dimension of baptism. In the early church,
when a convert was baptized he stood toward the West

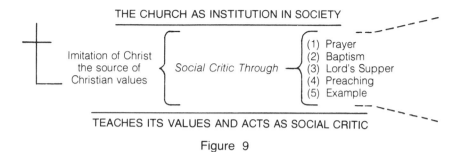

Figure 9

(the symbol of Satan's domain) and was asked by the minister, "Do you renounce Satan and all his works?" After the baptism, he would say, "I do," and spit in the direction of the West as a symbol of his total rejection of Satan and his power over his life. The church needs to recover this social implication of baptism and make it clearer to converts that to identify with Christ is to participate in his kingdom and to subscribe to all that this means.

The Lord's Supper also contains a radical social element. Because it is a re-enactment of Christ's death and resurrection, through which all evil has been put down, the sacrament is a constant reminder of the power of Christ over sin. Tissa Balasuriya argues in his book, *The Eucharist and Human Liberation,* that the early Christians understood the deep meaning of Communion and lived by its social impact. "That is why," he writes, "the early Christians were so acceptable to many, especially the poor, and so detested by some of the powerful, particularly the exploiters."[23] Certainly the Lord's Table speaks to us about human selfishness and human exploitation. It exposes the inequality of society and calls us to a radically new perception and lifestyle.

Preaching is another way in which the institutional church can make its impact. If preaching is to build the body of Christ, it must relate to our life in the world. Vermont Royster states it well:

> I cannot share the idea that preachers have no right, moral or otherwise, to raise their voices or that "religion has no place in politics." It has been part of American politics from the beginning. Pulpit voices played a role in making our revolution. They sounded loud and clear in their moral indignation at slavery and at those in politics who countenanced it. Their influence helped pass the 13th Amendment, which abolished it.[24]

Finally, the institutional church must set an example in the use of its own resources. William Stringfellow, lawyer and social critic, tells the story of a minister who asked what he could do about a family that had just been evicted from their apartment and had no money to buy food. Stringfellow told him, "Sell your tapestry." The point is well taken. The church too frequently looks after itself—its buildings, its parking lot, its furnishings—while the needs of hungry and oppressed people are neglected in the shadow of the steeple.

Here then are ways in which the institutional church can witness to the power of Christ over evil without entering into an unholy alliance with current economic or political powers. Now what can the church as the people of God do?

The People of God in Society

It is obvious that the church is fleshed out in society through people. In this sense the church must be seen as something more than an institution. It is people who constitute the body of Christ, who live and act within society as "salt" and "light." There are four avenues through which Christians can accomplish their calling.

First, Christians must never back away from the priority of personal evangelism. Christianity is a

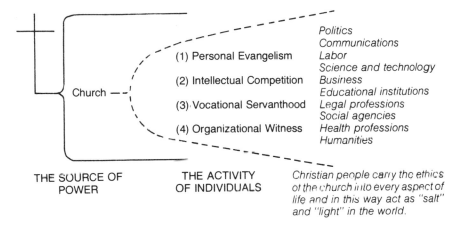

Figure 10

missionary movement. From the very beginning its goal has been to call on people to repent, to believe in Jesus, and to enter the life of the church. Those who come into the church are then taught by the church (as we have seen above) and go into the world to witness to Christ's power over evil.

But we must avoid the error that personal evangelism consists in passing out a tract or giving a witness. Secular man is not attracted to approaches that stand "outside" his suffering. People must be reached *where they are.* If we cannot share the suffering, the pain, the anxiety, and the boredom as well as the accomplishments, the joys, and the interests of the common secular man, then we will never reach him.

If all secular man ever sees in our lives and witness is negativism against women, or condemnation of homosexuals, or tirades against television morality and public education, he will remain untouched. What attracts people is a genuine love and compassion for people, a sincere desire to be a loyal friend, a willingness to give something of ourselves for another. What attracted sinners to Jesus was not his condemnation of their sin, but the genuine love and compassion he had for them—a love that took him to the cross and death. He is the model for our contact with people and for the methods we use to attract them into the kingdom.

Second, the people of God must enter into the marketplace of ideas and wrestle with the secular minds of the age. Christianity claims to be a "worldview." As such, it has a distinct view about the origin, meaning, and destiny of life. Christians must be willing to put forth the intellectual content of these ideas in the university centers of the world. Charles Malik, a former president of the United Nations, said, "No civilization can endure with its mind being as confused and disordered as ours is today. All our ills stem proximately from the false philosophies that have been let loose in the world and that are now being taught in the universities."[25]

But Christians must avoid an anti-intellectual spirit that disdains openness to inquiry and closes the door to discussion. It doesn't help the cause of Christ for Christians to make sweeping statements about humanists without a knowledge of what humanism is, where it came from, or what its present classifications are. It doesn't help the cause of Christianity when Christians act as though the Bible is a textbook for science, psychology, and sociology. It doesn't help the Christian cause to reject the legitimate pursuit of empirical studies in the natural or behavioral sciences and the humanities. It doesn't help the Christian faith to dismiss Socrates, Plato, Aristotle, or modern philosophers peremptorily as "decadent humanists." How can we expect anyone to listen to us when we speak out of ignorance, expressing a clear bias and a mere caricature of their viewpoint? If we really believe truth will triumph in the end, why don't we put our faith to the challenge and enter the intellectual citadels of the world?

Third, Christians must carry their convictions and values into their vocational callings and turn their vocations into opportunities for service. If the role of the Christian in the world is not success, power, prestige, or wealth, then Christians may and ought to use their talents and gifts in ways that will serve the world. There is no legitimate vocation that is closed to the Christian. The people of God are found everywhere —in politics, in the health professions, in social service, in blue-collar and white-collar jobs. It is here—on the job—that Christians must demonstrate through word and deed their ultimate commitment to Christ as Lord.

Bishop L. T. Matthiesen of the Roman Catholic diocese in Amarillo, Texas, in a noteworthy example, recently prodded Christian employees of the Pentax plant to quit their jobs. The plant is the nation's final assembly point for the neutron bomb. "We urge those involved in the production and stock piling of nuclear bombs," Matthiesen said, "to consider what they are doing, to resign from such activities, and to seek employment in peaceful pursuits."[26] The point is that Christians need to be more willing to act prophetically in their vocations.

Fourth, there is no reason why Christians cannot organize for the purposes of witness and impact on culture. There are already numerous parachurch organizations in education, welfare and social services, medical clinics, hunger and relief programs, morally concerned groups, and political lobbies. As long as the distinction between the role of the church as an institution and the people of God is maintained, there is no biblical or constitutional reason why Christians cannot exercise influence in the political, moral, social, or educational spheres of life.

This raises the issue of whether or not it is advisable for Christian people to ban together in an explicitly political organization such as the Moral Majority. Certainly there is nothing in Scripture that forbids Christians from organizing for political *service.* With regard to the Moral Majority, however, two weaknesses are evident. The first is that it is not explicitly Christian. Anyone, regardless of personal religious background or lack of it, may participate in the Moral Majority as long as his or her viewpoint on the issues is the same. It would be better for Christians to form a group that is explicitly Christian as a witness to Christian values, rather than an organization which has as its stated goals a defense of morality. By removing itself from a Christian base—by separating morals from their Christian roots—the Moral Majority has bought into the process of secularization.

The second problem with the Moral Majority is that it does not advocate a full Christian agenda. Its support of militarism is the most glaring example. In addition, its failure to speak out on behalf of the poor, the oppressed, and the downtrodden and its identification with wealth, success, and political power characterize it more as an organization for the promotion of the status quo, than an organization that wants to serve the needs of all the people. Regardless, it must be admitted that the Moral Majority has raised important issues for Christians and is in this way forcing us to look at old questions in a new context.

When Christians organize to serve the world, it is imperative that they avoid all attempts to change society through manipulative means, coercive measures, and censorship. The church is not to act as though everyone is to bow to its demands and follow its teachings through the imposition of law. The work of the church is always the path of invitation and persuasion, not legislation or coercion. In this respect the words of

Napoleon are quite appropriate. "Do you know what astounds me about the world?" Napoleon asked in his later days. "It is the impotence of force to establish anything . . . in the end the sword is always conquered by the mind."

CONCLUSION

It should be quite obvious by now that the church has an important and significant role to play in society. It is a means by which evil is restrained and the good is promoted.

These are the main points to remember about the role of the church in a secular society:

- The task of the church in the world is not accomplished through alliances with political and economic systems.

- The church as an institution must teach its values and act as a social critic in its life of prayer, baptism, the Lord's Supper, preaching, and lifestyle example. In this way the believer is prepared to live in the world.

- Individual Christians (or organized groups) take the values of the church and its world-view into all aspects of life through their vocational calling.

- The struggle with secular humanism and other expressions of secularization will continue to express itself in one way or another until the end of history.

One final haunting question remains. What can the church hope to accomplish? Can it change the world? Will it redeem the structures of society? Will it usher in a golden era of peace and brotherhood?

The biblical, theological, and historical answer to this question is both pessimistic and optimistic. On the pessimistic side, the church will always exist alongside fallen society in a tension that will vary from time to time and place to place. In certain times and places the church may be favored, at other times it will only be tolerated, and in still other times and places it will be persecuted and maligned. Evil continues to be a very powerful force in the world, because (although defeated by the Cross) it has yet to be utterly destroyed by the Consummation. So evil will rage and lash out within society and against the church to mock the Cross and malign the Creator and Redeemer of the universe.

So what is the church to do? Witness! It is to witness to what it knows will surely occur—that God in the time of his own choosing will deal an ultimate and decisive blow to evil, utterly destroying and banishing it forever. This is the optimistic face of the church.

Consequently we must see the threat of secular humanism as only one of many bold attempts of the doomed powers of evil to regain a footing in the world. The Cross declares that evil hasn't a chance of victory. Its defeat has already occurred, and its doom is imminent.

Thus the challenge of the church is not to change the world or "clean up America" or control the powers of evil through political or legislative means. The challenge of the church is to witness—to tell and to live out the good news that sin in all its forms has been conquered, to invite people into Christ and his church. Here, in Christ and his church, we engage in a continuing struggle with evil, knowing that the ultimate outcome has been determined, and live in the sure hope that Christ is victor!

The struggle in every aspect of life—personal, social, political, academic, vocational—is the arena in which the church witnesses to the ultimate victory over sin that only God can accomplish when he comes to consummate his work in Jesus Christ.

The struggle against the powers of evil must not and cannot cease. If it does, the witness of the church against evil will cease.

So rise up, O church, and let your voice and life be heard and felt.

Notes

CHAPTER 1

[1]Tim LaHaye, *The Battle for the Mind* (Old Tappan, N.J.: Revell, 1979), p. 10.

[2]Homer Duncan, *Secular Humanism* (Lubbock, Tex.: Missionary Crusader, 1979). The phrase "The most dangerous religion in America" is the subtitle of the book.

[3]Francis A. Schaeffer, *A Christian Manifesto* (Westchester, Ill.: Crossway Books, 1981), p. 17

[4]Thomas Molnar, *Christian Humanism: A Critique of the Secular City and Its Ideology* (Chicago: Franciscan Herald Press, 1978), p. 3.

[5]*Harvard University Gazette* (June 8, 1978).

[6]"De Descriptione Temporum" in *Selected Literary Essays* (Cambridge: Cambridge Univ. Press, 1969), p. 5.

[7]Bernard E. Meland, *The Secularization of Modern Cultures* (New York: Oxford Univ. Press, 1966), pp. 3, 16, 75.

[8]*Facing Up to Modernity* (New York: Basic Books, 1977), pp. 191-92.

CHAPTER 2

[1]Charles Krauthammer, "The Humanist Phantom," in *New Republic* (July 25, 1981):21.

[2]Quoted by Russell Chandler, "Humanists, Target of the Moral Right," in the *Los Angeles Times* (July 16, 1981).

[3]Krauthammer, "The Humanist Phantom," p. 21.

[4]"Humanism," World Book Encyclopedia, 1970, vol. 9, p. 385.

[5]C. Hassell Bullock, *An Introduction to the Poetic Books* (Chicago: Moody Press, 1979), p. 256.

[6]"Christianity and Humanistic Values in Eighteenth-Century America: A Bicentennial Review," in *Christian Scholar's Review*, vol. 6, nos. 2-3 (1976):114-15.

[7]Molnar, *Christian Humanism*, p. 4.

[8]*Didache*. See Cyril C. Richardson, ed., *Early Christian Fathers*,

Library of Christian Classics, vol. 1 (Philadelphia: Westminster Press, 1953), p. 172.

[9]*Apology.* See the *Ante-Nicene Fathers,* 1.15 (Grand Rapids: Eerdmans, 1971).

[10]"An Epistle to Diognetus," in Richardson, *Early Christian Fathers.*

[11]Crane Brinton, *The Shaping of Modern Thought* (Englewood Cliffs, N.J.: Prentice-Hall, 1963), p. 38.

[12]See "Humanism and the Moral Revolution," in *The Humanist Alternative,* ed. Paul Kurtz (Buffalo: Prometheus Books, 1973), pp. 49ff.

[13]Quoted by Y. H. Kirkorian, *Naturalism and the Human Spirit* (New York: Columbia Univ. Press, 1944), p. 382.

[14]*Los Angeles Times* (July 16, 1981).

[15]"Ethics and Humanist Imagination," in Kurtz, *The Humanist Alternative,* pp. 169ff.

[16]"Scientific Humanism," in Kurtz, *The Humanist Alternative,* pp. 109ff.

[17]"The Humanist Outlook," in Kurtz, *The Humanist Alternative,* pp. 133ff.

[18]*Hawkeye,* vol. 13, no. 8 (1981).

[19]*Eternity* (January 1982).

[20]Ignatius, *Letter to the Smyrneans,* chs. 6-7.

[21]*Hawkeye,* vol. 13, no. 8.

[22]Krauthammer, "The Humanist Phantom," p. 25.

CHAPTER 3

[1]See Kurtz, *The Humanist Alternative,* for some definitions of humanism.

[2]*A Secular Humanist Declaration* (Buffalo: Prometheus Books, 1980).

[3]Quotations are from an interview by Kenneth A. Briggs, published under the heading "Secular Humanists Attack a Rise in Fundamentalism," in the *New York Times* (October 1980).

[4]Ibid.

[5]*A Secular Humanist Declaration,* pp. 10-11.

[6]Ibid.

[7]Ibid., p. 12.

[8]"Judaism Under the Secular Umbrella," in *Christianity Today* (September 8, 1979):20.

[9]*A Secular Humanist Declaration,* p. 13.

[10]Ibid., pp. 14-16.

[11]Ibid., pp. 16-17.

[12]Ibid., p. 17.

[13]Ibid., pp. 17-18.

[14]Ibid.

[15]Ibid., pp. 19-20.

[16]"On the Uncertainty of Science," in *Harvard Magazine* (September-October 1980):20.

[17]*A Secular Humanist Declaration*, p. 21

[18]Ibid., pp. 21-22.

[19]Ibid., pp. 22-23.

[20]Ibid.

[21]*Harvard University Gazette* (June 8, 1978).

[22]Quoted by Charles Krauthammer, "The Humanist Phantom," p. 25.

[23]*Harvard University Gazette* (June 8, 1978).

[24]Kurtz, *The Humanist Alternative*, pp. 51-52.

[25]June Goodfield, *Playing God* (New York: Harper & Row, 1977), p. 5.

CHAPTER 4

[1]*Chicago Statement Report* (Spring 1981).

[2]Ibid.

[3]Ibid.

[4]Ibid.

[5]Quoted by Daniel Hunninger, "What That Boycott Was About," in *The Wall Street Journal* (June 30, 1981).

[6]*His People* (October 1981):25.

[7]Ibid.

[8]Ibid.

[9]EP News Service (Fall 1981).

[10]"Sex Business Booms Despite Cleanup Drive," in *U.S. News & World Report* (March 16, 1981):56.

[11]*Chicago Tribune* (June 13, 1981).

[12]"Sex Business Booms Despite Cleanup Drive."

[13]Ibid.

[14]Ibid.

[15]Jerry Falwell, *Listen America* (New York: Doubleday, 1980), p. 236.

[16]Ibid., p. 229.

CHAPTER 5

[1]*Baptist Peacemaker*, vol. 1, no. 3.

[2]October 21, 1981.

[3]"Is 'The Deer Hunter' Movie Too Deadly for Television?" in the *Chicago Tribune* (November 17, 1981).

[4]"The Feds and the Family," in the *Washington Post* (September 3, 1980).

[5]See H. R. 311 of the 97th Congress, First Session.

[6]*Chicago Tribune* (November 14, 1981).

[7]"Child Abuse and Neglect in the American Society," in *The Center Magazine* (March-April 1978):72.

[8]Ibid., p. 74.

[9]Ibid., p. 76.

[10]EP News (September 12, 1981):9-10.

[11]"A Doctor's Viewpoint," in *Good News* (July-August 1976).

CHAPTER 6

[1]LaHaye, *The Battle for the Mind*, p. 167.

[2]*Chicago Tribune* (November 21, 1971).

[3]Ibid.

[4]"Justice for Education," pamphlet (Washington, D.C.: Association for Public Justice).

[5]Ibid.

[6]*Christianity Today* (April 10, 1981):45.

[7]*His*, Denver (October 1981).

[8]Ibid.

[9]*Newsweek* (September 1980).

[10]Quoted by George Will, "Sex and the Single Mind." Washington Post Writers Group.

[11]*Newsweek* (September 1980).

[12]Will, "Sex and the Single Mind."

[13]"Teacher Sex Guide," in the *Los Angeles Times* (March 26, 1980).

[14]EP News (November 1, 1980):8.

[15]"Scopes II in California," in *Newsweek* (March 16, 1981).

[16]*Science*, vol. 209 (September 12, 1980).

[17]*Publishers Weekly* (June 12, 1981).

[18]Address to scientists and members of the Pontifical Academy of Sciences, October 3, 1981.

[19]James J. Kilpatrick, "The Useless Debate on Religious Tokenism,"

in the *Los Angeles Times* (August 14, 1980). Universal Press Syndicate.

²⁰The Establishment Clause is part of the First Amendment: "Congress shall make no law respecting an establishment of religion, or prohibiting the free exercise thereof." The decision also alludes to the next clause: "or abridging the freedom of speech, or of the press."

²¹*Chicago Tribune* (December 1981).

CHAPTER 7

¹*Newsweek* (September 15, 1980).

²Ibid.

³*Time* (September 4, 1981):28.

⁴Paper delivered at the Conference on Liberty and Equality in America at the University of Houston, April 21, 1979.

⁵Ibid.

⁰Ibid.

⁷Ibid.

⁸Oscar Cullmann, *The State in the New Testament* (New York: Scribner's, 1956), p. 3. Emphasis added.

⁹EP News Service.

¹⁰Cullmann, *The State in the New Testament*, p. 63.

¹¹Ibid.

¹²Ibid., pp. 73-74.

CHAPTER 8

¹"Triumph of the Moral Majority and disaffection of Institutional Christians," distributed by Urban Consultants, Rochester, N.Y.

²Duncan, *Secular Humanism*, p. 38.

³EP News (August 1, 1981):8.

⁴*Christian Scholar's Review*, vol. 6, nos. 2-3 (1976):114-16.

⁵Ibid., p. 115.

⁶Ibid., p. 116.

⁷Ibid., p. 117.

⁸Ibid., p. 118.

⁹Ibid., p. 121.

¹⁰Ibid., pp. 122-24.

¹¹Falwell, *Listen America*, pp. 21-22.

¹²Ibid., p. 29.

¹³EP News (October 1980):1.

[14]Box 26111, San Jose, California.

[15]*Christianity Today* (September 8, 1981):25.

[16]Quoted in "Are We All God's People?" pamphlet distributed by People for the American Way.

[17]*Parade* (September 1981).

[18]"Are We All God's People?"

[19]Ibid.

[20]*Christianity Today* (September 8, 1981):27.

[21]EP News Service.

[22]*The Wall Street Journal*, n.d.

[23]Tissa Balasuriya, *The Eucharist and Human Liberation* (New York: Orbis Books, 1977), p. 25.

[24]*The Wall Street Journal*, n.d.

[25]Charles Malik, *The Two Tasks* (Westchester, Ill.: Crossway Books, 1980).

[26]*The Christian Century* (September 9, 1981):857.

Bibliography

I. THE RELIGIOUS RIGHT

Duncan, Homer. *Secular Humanism*. Lubbock, Tex: Missionary Crusader, 1979.

Falwell, Jerry. *Listen America*. New York: Doubleday, 1980.

Helms, Jesse. *When Free Men Shall Stand*. Grand Rapids: Zondervan, 1976.

LaHaye, Tim. *The Battle for the Mind*. Old Tappan, N.J.: Fleming H. Revell, 1979.

Robison, James and Cox, Jim. *Save America to Save the World*. Wheaton, Ill: Tyndale, 1980.

Schaeffer, Francis A. *A Christian Manifesto*. Westchester, Ill.: Crossway Books, 1981.

II. ON SECULARIZATION

Berger, Peter. *Facing Up to Modernity*. New York: Basic Books, 1977.

———. *The Noise of Solemn Assemblies*. New York: Doubleday, 1961.

———. *The Precarious Vision*. New York: Doubleday, 1967.

———. *The Sacred Canopy*. New York: Doubleday, 1967.

Childress, James F., and Harned, David B., eds. *Secularization and the Protestant Perspective*. Philadelphia: Westminster Press, 1970.

Durkheim, Emile. *The Elementary Forms of the Religious Life*. New York: Free Press, 1965.

Greeley, Andrew M. *Unsecular Man: The Persistence of Religion*. New York: Schocken, 1972.

Martin, David. *A General Theory of Secularization*. New York: Harper & Row, 1978.

Meland, Bernard E. *The Secularization of Modern Cultures*. New York: Oxford Univ. Press, 1966.

III. HUMANISM

Blackham, Harold J., ed. *Objections to Humanism.*
Westport, Conn.: Greenwood Press, 1974.
Coates, Willson H. *The Emergence of Liberal Humanism.*
New York: McGraw-Hill, 1966.
Ehrenfeld, David. *The Arrogance of Humanism.* New York:
Oxford, 1978.
Humanist Manifesto I & II. Buffalo: Prometheus Books,
1973.
Kurtz, Paul, ed. *The Humanist Alternative.* Buffalo: Prom-
etheus Books, 1973.
_____. ed. *Moral Problems in Contemporary Society.* Buf-
falo: Prometheus Books, 1973.
A Secular Humanist Declaration. Buffalo: Prometheus
Books, 1981.
Storer, Morris B., ed. *Humanist Ethics.* Buffalo: Prom-
etheus Books, 1980.

IV. CHRISTIAN HUMANISM

Allen, Edgar L. *Christian Humanism: A Guide to the
Thought of Jacques Maritain.* London: Hodder &
Stoughton, 1950.
Barcus, Nancy B. *Developing A Christian Mind.* Downers
Grove, Ill.: InterVarsity Press, 1977.
Breen, Quirinus. *Christianity and Humanism.* Grand
Rapids: Eerdmans, 1968.
Brown, Colin. *Philosophy and the Christian Faith.*
Wheaton: Tyndale, 1969.
Holmes, Arthur. *All Truth Is God's Truth.* Grand Rapids:
Eerdmans, 1977.
_____. *Faith Seeks Understanding.* Grand Rapids:
Eerdmans, 1971.
Johnson, Robert L. *Humanism and Beyond.* Philadelphia:
United Church Press, 1973.
Maritain, Jacques. *Integral Humanism: Temporal and
Spiritual Problems of a New Humanism.* Notre Dame,
Ind.: Univ. Notre Dame Press, 1973.
_____. *True Humanism.* Westport, Conn.: Greenwood
Press, 1970.
_____. *The Twilight of Civilization.* London: Sheed & Ward,
1946.

Martin, Janet-Kerr. *The Secular Promise: Christian Humanism Amid Contemporary Humanism.* Philadelphia: Westminster Press, 1964.

Molnar, Thomas. *Christian Humanism.* Chicago: Franciscan Herald Press, 1978.

Shinn, Roger. *Man: The New Humanism.* Philadelphia: Westminster Press, 1968.

Strawson, William. *The Christian Approach to the Humanist.* London: Lutterworth Press, 1970.

V. CHRISTIAN RESPONSIBILITY IN SOCIETY

Scott, Waldron. *Bring Forth Justice.* Grand Rapids: Eerdmans, 1980.

Skillen, James W. *Christians Organizing for Political Service.* Washington, D.C.: Association for Public Justice, 1980.

Niebuhr, Richard. *Christ and Culture.* New York: Harper, 1951.

Webber, Robert E. *The Moral Majority: Right or Wrong?* Westchester, Ill.: Crossway Books, 1981.

_____. *The Secular Saint.* Grand Rapids: Zondervan, 1979.

Webster, Douglas D. *Christian Living in a Pagan Culture.* Wheaton: Tyndale, 1980.

White, R. E. O. *Biblical Ethics.* Atlanta: John Knox, 1979.

_____. *Christian Ethics.* Atlanta: John Knox, 1981.